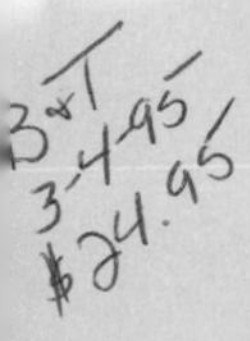

W9-CDC-324

DRIED FLOWER GIFTS

DRIED FLOWER GIFTS

CREATING DECORATIVE ARRANGEMENTS

STEPHANIE DONALDSON

PHOTOGRAPHY BY SHONA WOOD

ABBEVILLE PRESS • PUBLISHERS
New York • London • Paris

To Lena, Sally and Stewart, and Rose

First published in the United States of America in 1994 by
Abbeville Press, 488 Madison Avenue, New York, NY 10022

First published in the UK in 1994 by
New Holland (Publishers) Ltd
Chapel House, 24 Nutford Place,
London W1H 6DQ

Printed and bound in Hong Kong by South China Printing Company Ltd

ISBN 0-78920-005-8

First edition
2 4 6 8 10 9 7 5 3

Editorial direction Yvonne McFarlane
Editor Coral Walker
Art director Jane Forster
Illustrator Claire Davis
Design assistant Sarah Willis
Background artist and props Kathy Fillion Ritchie

Contents

Foreword

The very first thing I say to students when I am teaching dried flower workshops is 'I am totally untrained. I am not going to show you the *right* way to do things, I am going to show you *a* way which works for me and can work for you too'.

Once they have got over the shock of being addressed by a rank amateur, I explain that you don't need a qualification to have ideas, just the confidence to try them out. Like my workshops, this book is not about perfect technique, it's about learning to be creative and enjoying yourself.

Paul Klee the artist once said that drawing was 'taking a line for a walk'. I think of my creative work as 'taking an idea for a walk'. When I start working on a project I frequently have no inkling of where I will end up; instead I let the materials inspire me, my mood influence me and then give myself up to the creative process.

Having new ideas often involves taking risks, but it's only by trying something new and sometimes getting it wrong that we move forward. Even when things do go wrong, I don't abandon my disasters, I just put them out of sight for a while, then take another look at them and a solution nearly always presents itself. If nothing comes immediately to mind, I put the project away for a little longer and try again. After three weeks I generally accept that this particular idea has got hopelessly lost and keep it to prove to my students that I don't always get it right.

Students often say to me, 'Well its easy for you, you're so creative'. My reply to this is that yes, I do consider myself to be creative, but that this is an ability that I have developed, rather than a gift with which I was born. I firmly believe that we all have the potential to be 'creative' and I hope that this book will help you to discover your own latent talent, first by giving you step-by-step projects to follow, then later by encouraging you to step out and take your own ideas 'for a walk'.

Introduction

HISTORY OF DRIED FLOWERS

Today's books on dried flowers are full of wonderful decorative ideas, but the history of the subject is far removed from the decorative arts.

Since the very earliest times, civilised societies have used dried flowers for their aromatic and healing properties. The Egyptians used flowers, herbs and aromatics in their cosmetics, and entertained their guests in rooms fragranced with pot-pourri. Cleopatra welcomed her lover in an apartment that was strewn knee-deep with rose petals.

Both the Greeks and Romans continued this tradition by marking great occasions with showers of scented flowers, sometimes in such abundance that in ancient Rome a guest was asphyxiated.

All cultures have their traditions of healing herbs and flowers that have been passed down through the centuries. As Europe entered the Dark Ages and the great civilisations of Greece and Rome declined, it was left to the monks and the housewives to carry the knowledge.

In the Middle Ages it is likely that the majority of dried flowers were in fact fed to cattle and horses. The medieval hay meadows were a far cry from today's carefully cultivated pastures, and the abundant flowers that grew in these fields were as important as the grasses.

Housewives started to dry flowers and herbs for their aromatic and healing qualities and by the time that Elizabeth I ascended the throne of England, the stillroom was an important part of the house. Here, herbs and flowers hung to dry and the housewife would prepare herbal waters, pot-pourri, strewing herbs and innumerable lotions and potions. While the primary function of all these preparations was to promote health and ward off the evil stenches that were part of everyday life, there was a growing appreciation of the beauty of flowers. Decorative gardens were planted in Europe for the first time since the fall of Rome and an increasing variety of plants was brought from distant lands. Flowers no longer needed to be useful, their beauty was sufficient.

Over the centuries, this appreciation grew until it reached its apotheosis in Victorian times. Flowers were everywhere. Vast teams of gardeners tended elaborate gardens and cossetted exotic blossoms in conservatories. Cutting gardens were established to keep the house supplied with fresh blooms and, significantly for this book, dried flowers or 'immortelles' as they were then known were an important crop.

The flowers dried by the Victorians are familiar to us today. They include statice, *Helichrysum*, achillea, honesty and Chinese lanterns as well as the aromatic herbs, all of which air dry quite readily. The Victorian ladies spent many hours making intricate tussie-mussies, or waxing flowers for display under glass domes; nothing was too time consuming, for they had little else to do.

With the arrival of the twentieth century all this changed. People had busy lives, the gardeners were gone and dried flower arranging was relegated to a minor craft for Women's Institutes.

Looking back, it seems to me that in my youth most of my aged relatives possessed at least one dried flower arrangement. It was nearly always in a fireplace, a sad concoction of faded statice, honesty and Chinese lanterns festooned with dust. I thought they were hideous and would have greeted the information that I would one day write a book on the subject with utter disbelief.

Left: A quick and easy idea for a rustic table decoration: this simple candle rises from a ruff of bay leaves and chilli peppers. Right: Dresser tops and doorways look wonderful when decorated with swags. The hydrangeas and achillea are simply wired on to a hay rope.

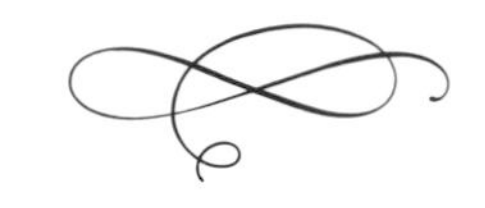

The fact that I am now writing this book is due to the renaissance that dried flowers have undergone in the last fifteen years. New designers have shown us that dried flowers can be a desirable and attractive alternative to fresh flowers rather than a second-rate substitute. Modern technology has greatly improved drying and storage techniques so that the huge variety of flowers that we buy today last better, keep their colour longer and more closely resemble their fresh counterparts.

BUYING DRIED FLOWERS

These days few of us have the space or the time to grow sufficient dried flowers in our own gardens, so it is important that when we buy flowers we know what to look for.

I have an aversion to dyed dried flowers and never use them. But avoiding dyed flowers does not mean that your palette will be limited. Flip through the pages of this book and you will see a rainbow of colour. Flowers that have been well dried and stored will have wonderful rich colours, often deeper than when they were freshly picked. True, they will fade with time, but this is a gradual process and most dried flower arrangements retain a good colour for one to two years provided that they are not displayed in direct sunlight.

Ideally, you should buy your dried flowers from a grower or a specialist shop which carries large stocks and has a quick turnover. Dried flowers are quite fragile and the more they are handled

the more likely they are to be damaged. When you buy from a grower, the flowers will have been picked, dried and stored in optimum conditions. They will not have been thrown around in transit, displayed for some time and handled by customers, so you will have a far better chance of buying a bunch of flowers that is in peak condition. Similarly, a specialist shop will ensure that the flowers are properly handled and stored.

The best dried flowers are not cheap, but compared with fresh flowers they are very good value for money.

GETTING STARTED

For those who have never tried dried flower arranging before, this is the exciting part. You have the book, the flowers and now you are ready to start. I should now propound my theories on colour and form, but I would like to tell you a story about myself instead.

In my late teens, I met a group of keen bridge players who persuaded me to join them. I played quite well and thoroughly enjoyed myself until one evening, when having trounced our opponents, my

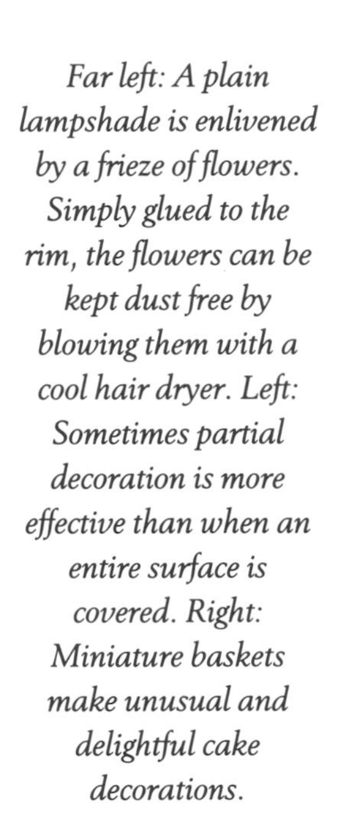

Far left: A plain lampshade is enlivened by a frieze of flowers. Simply glued to the rim, the flowers can be kept dust free by blowing them with a cool hair dryer. Left: Sometimes partial decoration is more effective than when an entire surface is covered. Right: Miniature baskets make unusual and delightful cake decorations.

partner proceeded to explain to them why I had played my cards the way I did, what conventions I had followed and what my bids had told him. I was amazed because what he attributed to a sound understanding of the rules of bridge was in fact pure intuition.

Similarly, when it comes to colour and form, I *feel* what to do rather than follow any rules. The exciting part about doing it this way is that you will, in time, discover the rules for yourself, you will notice that certain colours used together are intensified, that some proportions work better than others and that rules are only other people's observations.

Observation is the key to all creativity. I am a careful observer of everything around me and would recommend that you develop this ability in yourself. There are so many inspirations in everyday life, some in the most surprising places – it may be the colour and texture of a tree trunk, a photograph in a magazine or a cleverly decorated shop window. Stop and look closer, see if you can put your finger on what it was that attracted you, and make a mental note.

For example, a few months ago I saw a wonderful Chinese film. The story takes place in rural China in the middle of winter with little colour in the landscape but the outsides of the peasants houses are hung with festoons of chillis and corn hung to dry under the eaves. The intensity of the reds and yellows against the drab countryside made an indelible impression on me and I have carried that image in my mind ever since.

So inspiration is all around us. We live in a world of colour, form and texture and, once you develop the habit of observation, you will find a never ending source of new ideas.

I called into one of my suppliers recently to pick up some materials for the projects in this book and, as usual, I wandered round looking at what was new. Two items caught my eye, a divided picture frame and a tiny woven basket. At that stage I had no idea what I would do with them, but I brought them home and put them on a shelf in my workroom. A few days later I was sent a sample of tiny yellow rosebuds and it occurred to me that they would look good in the picture frame alongside other flowers and some mosses, so I

Above: These little display boxes are readily available and look exquisite filled with a selection of colours and textures. They are also the perfect way to use up leftover pieces. Left: A whimsical display of dahlias, hydrangeas and oak leaves adorn an iron candelabra.

Tiny posies transform a gift into something really special. Select flowers of complementary hues and tuck the stems into the ribbon or tie.

played around with the idea and found it worked. I shall buy more frames and experiment further. The little basket came in useful when I was icing a cake and felt too lazy to walk to the shops to buy decorations. Casting around for a substitute, the little basket came to hand, and filled with little roses and moss it makes a very pretty decoration and a charming keepsake.

Don't feel that you should restrict the use of dried flowers to 'arrangements', they have many other decorative uses within the home. A simple coolie lampshade is enlivened with an edging of dried flowers and a picture frame is transformed by mosses and shells.

For a special occasion such as a wedding, decorate a hat with a garland of dried flowers and make a brooch to match. Gifts look even better with a few dried flowers tucked into the ribbon.

When I first started working with dried flowers I, too, bought books and followed other people's ideas. As you work on the projects in this book you will gain confidence in your own abilities and by emulating my style you will work towards the point where your own begins to develop. If you are a beginner, choose an easy project like a lavender posy on page 20 or the Victorian rose pot on page 52 before moving on to something more ambitious.

I hope that this book will help open the door to your creativity and be a source of inspiration and enjoyment.

Posies

I love giving and receiving fresh flowers, but experience has taught me that as delighted as I am with a lovely bunch of flowers, it is hard to give it the attention it needs when I am greeting guests or preparing a meal. A dried flower posy is an ideal alternative. Lavender is my favourite. With its intense colour and heady scent it seems that no one can resist its charms and, appropriately presented, it makes a suitable gift in most situations. Decorate a little bunch with tiny roses and tie the posy together with a sumptuous bow – it can grace the most elegant drawing room. A more austere treatment, using simple cord to bind the lavender, creates a modern effect which will look striking in contemporary surroundings.

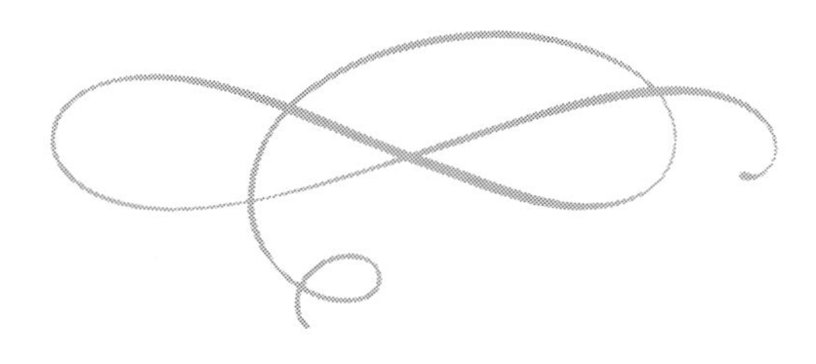

The posy has always been popular and in the past its function was rightly believed to be therapeutic as well as decorative. In medieval Europe bunches of aromatic herbs were carried in the belief that they helped ward off the plague. The essential oils contained in the herbs are indeed powerful germicides, but the amounts present in the posies were not sufficient to deal with the filth and disease of medieval life.

In Victorian times, where all was circumspection when it came to the emotions, a highly complex Language of Flowers was developed to allow lovers and friends to communicate their feelings to one another. The 'tussie-mussie' was hugely popular, with concentric circles of brightly coloured flowers assembled to carry highly significant messages. For example, a posy of forget-me-nots, single pinks and ivy would signify pure, true love and hopes of marriage. But woe betide a careless lover should the pink show some variegation in its flower, for then the posy would convey a message of refusal.

Visit any rural French market and, like me, you will be charmed by elderly ladies selling delightful posies made of cottage garden flowers. Great care goes into the selection of the flowers for these posies and the skill with which they are assembled is an inspiration and something I try to emulate when making my own posies.

Dried flower posies have the added advantage of longevity and will remain as a memento of a happy evening for many months after the event.

With highly aromatic flowers there is an inherent fragrance which adds to the

pleasure. With less fragrant flowers, I add sachets of pot-pourri to impart that extra dimension.

In this chapter you will find a variety of posies to make. You can follow the projects exactly to achieve a copy of the posy shown, or you can take inspiration from the ideas and use them to create a posy of your own.

When I was asked by a museum to devise a gift to commemorate the opening of their new herb garden, I decided that a posy of dried herbs would be most appropriate. You can see this design on page 31. The soft greys, pinks and purples of the herbs are emphasized by the subtle tones of the tartan ribbon used to bind the posy.

One of the loveliest qualities of the lavender posy on page 20 is that it releases its wonderful fragrance each time it is touched. In aromatherapy, lavender is one of the great healers, as well as having calming and mood-lifting qualities, so not only will you be giving a gift that looks good, it will also be doing good. It is an ideal gift for a friend in hospital or an elderly relative.

And if you are feeling ambitious, why not attempt the Victorian tussie-mussie on page 24. This attractive combination of herbs and flowers emits a long-lasting fragrance from a series of lacy sachets which are incorporated into the design.

On dark winter evenings, when the flowers of summer seem impossibly far off, I will gather together a selection of flowers and happily assemble a number of posies. Once made, I wrap each posy in tissue paper and put them away in a cardboard box to wait until such time as I feel I wish to use them.

Posies can be so versatile, from the rich combination of ingredients in the Victorian posy (left) to the relative simplicity of the Country posy (right).

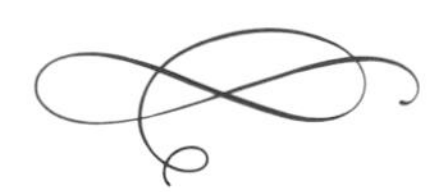

Lavender posy

I have decorated the posy described below with little spray roses. Numbers of the tiny blooms are carried on a single stem, so two or three stems are all that is needed to complete the effect. Take time and experiment with the placing of the flowers so that their softening effect on the rather rigid lavender is at its best. Be aware of scale when you work with dried flowers, as very different effects can be created this way. For instance, if you decide to vary this design and use three large roseheads instead of the little spray roses, and tie the posy with cord instead of ribbon, the result will be very different.

The simple symmetry of these lavender posies is enhanced by the different finishing touches. Hang them from door handles to scent your home and every time a door is opened a little of the fragrance will be released. Even when the flowers start to fade, don't throw them away but use them in a linen cupboard or a box of treasured letters where they will continue to emit their subtle fragrance.

The bunches of lavender you obtain from your supplier will generally be large enough to make two posies. I have discovered that a well-proportioned posy uses a bundle of lavender I can hold in one hand.

It is worth taking some time to get all the flowerheads at the same level as it creates a richer, denser effect in the finished posy. You will notice that in most bundles of lavender the flowerheads are uneven, many of them hidden by the stems of other flowers and you will lose the full impact of the flowers and their rigid architectural quality unless you spend a bit of time correcting this. Step 1 explains the easiest way to prepare the lavender and show it to its best advantage. If you have an open fireplace, do keep any trimmings, as they will scent the room with the fragrance of summer when thrown on the fire.

Variations:
The photograph shows you the extraordinarily different effects that can be achieved using a simple lavender posy as a starting point. The softly romantic lavender and roses, the rustic country decoration using a large raffia bow, the stark simplicity of the cord tie with the single *Nigella* seedhead and the lavish flourish of beautiful ribbons – all enhance the simple beauty of the lavender and demonstrate the versatility of the technique.

MATERIALS

Lavender
3 stems little spray roses
garden string or raffia
75 cm (30 in) ribbon 50 mm (2in) wide

Left: a silk tartan bow tied with deep blue satin ribbon complements the natural colour of the lavender. Right: little pink roses encircle the basic posy. You could use roses of a different hue: a pale yellow or a deeper red would both work well.

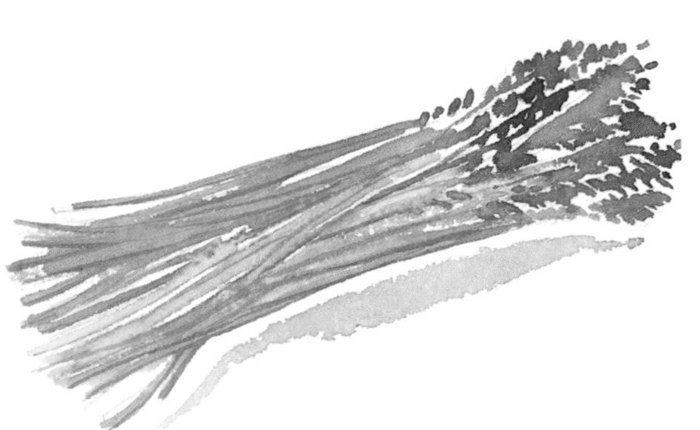

1 First prepare the bundle of lavender. Take about 10 stems of lavender at a time and hold them loosely in your hand with the heads resting on a table top. Gently shake them until all the heads are touching the table, then add another 10 heads and repeat the process, continuing until you have a large enough bundle for your posy.

2 Tie the bundle of lavender halfway down the stems with string or raffia. Knot the string or raffia and trim it neatly – this does not need to be decorative as you will cover it with ribbon or cord later. Trim the end of the stems so that they are all the same length.

Your choice of tie will completely alter the final effect. Compare the bright cerise moiré ribbon with this simple cord (left). Raffia is a versatile material (right). It can be plaited, twisted, tied in a simple knot or a luxurious bow.

3 Place the tiny roses on the posy with each flowerhead at a different level, so that the roses are shown off to the best effect. Tie firmly in place with the ribbon and leave tails of about 15 cm (6 in). Trim the stems of the roses level with the lavender stems.

4 Take another length of ribbon, approximately 45 cm (18 in) long and fold it in three. Pinch it in the middle and tie it to the bundle using the ribbon tails already attached. Tease out the bow and trim the ribbon tails at an angle to finish off the posy. If you wish, you can sew a small brass or plastic ring to the ribbon at the back of the posy, so that it can be hung up and displayed.

Victorian posy

While many of my designs have a contemporary appearance, this aromatic nosegay of herbs and flowers is unashamedly nostalgic. Known as a tussie-mussie, this enchanting little posy would find a place in any Victorian lady's boudoir. Decorative scented sachets have been incorporated into the design to ensure an enduring fragrance.

This pretty posy could be made to mark a special occasion: soft pastels for the birth of a baby, flowers symbolic of love for an engagement, or appropriately coloured foliage for an anniversary.

Making a tussie-mussie is a little more complicated than some of the other projects, and I would recommend that you get a feel for the different flowers and materials by making some simple posies before you embark on this one.

In Elizabethan times the courtiers of England carried tussie-mussies to ward off diseases. In Victorian days, they would scent a lady's boudoir. Nowadays their function is purely decorative and they make delightful bridesmaids' posies to be cherished long after the event.

MATERIALS

Peony
10 *Nigelia orientalis* seedheads
4 stems little spray roses
Small bunch pink achillea
Few stems each marjoram, savory and artemesia
4 circles sheer/lace fabric 7.5 cm (3 in)
1 tbsp dried lavender flowers or 4 cotton wool balls
Lavender essential oil
Paper doily 19 cm (7½ in) diameter
Paper doily 22 cm (8½ in) diameter
Fine green florists' wire
4 pieces stub wire 15 cm (6 in) long
Green florists' tape
2 m (2 yd) ribbon 10 mm (½ in) wide

I have used a peony as my centrepiece. It creates a strong focal point with its rich colouring and densely-packed petals. Select one with a straight stem, roughly 20 cm (8 in) long. This central flower is surrounded by *Nigella orientalis*, which is a great favourite of mine. Its soft green colouring and wonderful architectural shape is both eye-catching and functional, because its strong, spiky seedheads protect the more delicate flowers from damage. This is encircled by little bunches of pink achilleas and tiny roses, alternating with the lacy scented sachets.

Unlike the most robust archilleas, the pink form has very fragmented flowerheads and I have found that a better effect is achieved when they are bunched together.

The scented sachets can be made from net but, in this case, I have used cream lace over contrast-

ing magenta voile, to complement the flowers. As the amount of fabric used is minimal, it is worth looking out for attractive remnants or antique scraps as it is these finishing touches which make an arrangement special. I have filled the sachets with lavender flowers enhanced with lavender oil, but you can simply use cotton wool scented with an aromatic oil.

Surrounding the achillea, roses and scented sachets is a circlet of marjoram, savory and silver artemesia. These are less rigid than the rest of the posy and gently soften the edges where they meet the ruff of paper doilies.

Each layer of flowers is wired into the nosegay as the design is built up. Don't try assembling the whole posy and then wiring the finishing object, as it is almost impossible to achieve a geometric effect this way, and you will be forced to keep it in one hand until it is finished!

I have used two different-sized paper doilies for the ruff and finally a toning ribbon to bind the stems and cover the florists' tape.

1 *Attach fine green wire firmly to the stem of the peony and wire the* Nigella *heads in a circle around the peony, binding the wire around the stems to about 13 cm (5 in) below the flowerheads.*

2 *Make up four tiny bunches of achillea and roses, binding them together with green wire.*

3 *Put a teaspoon of lavender, enriched with a drop of lavender oil, into the centre of each fabric circle. Bend a hook into one end of the stub wire and place this end into the centre of the fabric. Gather the fabric up and bind the sachet on to the wire stem using the fine green wire. Repeat this for the other sachets.*

4 *Position the sachets of lavender and the bunches of achillea and roses alternately around the* Nigella *and bind them into the tussie-mussie.*

5 *Add a mixed row of marjoram, savory and artemesia and bind wire firmly round the stems of all the flowers to finish. Trim the stems just below where the wire finishes.*

Seen in its profile, the Victorian posy displays its practical yet decorative ribbon-bound stem and paper ruff. If you are making this for a wedding, choose white or cream ribbon for the bride and a colour to coordinate with the bridesmaids' dresses.

6 Make two cuts 3 cm (1 in) long in the middle of both doilies and slip the smaller, then the larger doily over the stem of the tussie-mussie.

7 Cover the wired stems with green florists' tape, using the tape to hold the doilies in place. Complete the posy with the ribbon. Wind it round the taped stems, starting at the bottom and working upwards. Under the ruff, tie a bow, leaving long ribbon tails.

Country posy

The charm of this posy is its informality. As I selected the flowers, I imagined wandering through a meadow, picking flowers as I found them, and I have consciously avoided an 'arranged' effect. Consequently, this posy is less symmetrical than the others and you may need to experiment with the placing of the flowers.

MATERIALS

Achillea filipendulina
3 peonies
5 stems little spray roses
Wheat
Lavender
Fine reel wire or twine
50 cm (20 in) ribbon 15 mm (½ in–¾ in) wide

One of the nicest innovations at florists in recent years has been the introduction of the 'tied arrangement' which is ready to pop into a vase when you receive it. This posy is the dried flower equivalent, and because it is 'randomly' gathered, you might find it easier to position the flowers by filling a small container with damp sand and pushing the stems of the flowers into the sand which will hold them in place while you make adjustments. For more impact, add the wheat and lavender in little bundles rather than individually. Once you are happy with how the flowers look, the stems can be bound with wire before removing the posy from the sand. The sand will drop off as it dries and you can then add the finishing ruff of wheat and complete the posy with a simple bow.

The strong, hot colours of this vibrant posy combine with the ears of wheat to conjure up the hues of high summer. The rich yellow-ochre *Achillea filipendulina* or yarrow, is one of my favourite dried flowers. With its dense flowerheads of golden yellow, it combines wonderfully with the vivid pinks of the peonies and roses which in turn contrast with the deep blue of the lavender. The wheat offers a different texture and creates a ruff around the flowers.

It was a particularly cold, wet, winter's day when I made this posy and its glowing colours proved a wonderful antidote to the weather outside. This is a mood-improver, perfect for someone whose life needs brightening.

This posy is a riot of colour, mixing turmeric yellow, shocking pink and deep blue with soft green and all tied with yellow satin. It would make an eye-catching bouquet at an informal country wedding.

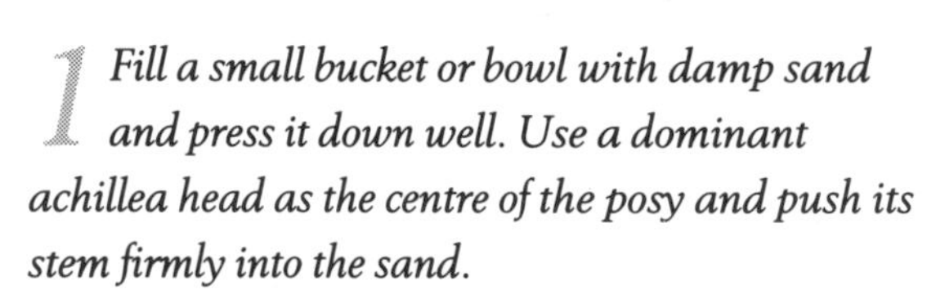

1 Fill a small bucket or bowl with damp sand and press it down well. Use a dominant achillea head as the centre of the posy and push its stem firmly into the sand.

2 Start to build up the arrangement round the central flower, making sure that all the stems are angled towards the centre. When you are happy with the placing of the flowers, bind the stems firmly together with wire or twine, just above the sand.

3 Pull the posy out of the sand and place it on a piece of newspaper to let the sand dry. It should fall off the stems; give the bunch a gentle shake to remove any stubborn grains.

4 Hold the posy in one hand and encircle the flowers with wheat to conceal the less decorative stems and create an attractive ruff. Bind the wheat firmly in place with wire or twine.

5 Trim the stems so that they are level. Tie a simple ribbon bow over the wire or twine to conceal it and complete the posy.

Herb posy

The soft colours of the herbs and their gentle fragrance makes them perfect candidates for an unusual posy of great subtlety. I have used flowering mint, artemesia, oregano, marjoram and sage tied with a tartan ribbon; but most herbs which dry successfully are suitable, and combine as well in a posy as in a cooking pot.

These posies make a lovely gift for a keen cook, as a thank you for a lovely dinner, although you might find friends reluctant to make use of the herbs if your culinary posies too pretty!

My garden is quite small, and I have to buy most of the dried flowers that I use; but I do grow and dry as many herbs as I can, so that I am surrounded by their fragrance throughout the year. Another important factor for cultivating my own herbs is that most of the commercially dried herbs sold alongside dried flowers have been fumigated, which makes them unsuitable for culinary use.

Herbs are extremely easy to dry. Wrapped in small bunches in newspaper cones to exclude light and dust and to stop the leaves curling, they can then be air dried in a warm spot. Alternatively, most herbs dry quickly and successfully in a microwave oven. (See drying techniques on page 119.)

This is a very simple posy to make, especially if you follow the instructions, and assemble and prepare the materials before you start working. This will ensure that you can put the whole posy together easily, without wiring each individual herb bunch separately.

Herbs destined for culinary use should not be those supplied for the dried flower market; these are often sprayed with dangerous pesticides.

MATERIALS

1 bunch each of:

flowering mint, artemesia, oregano, marjoram and sage (or similar herbs)

Fine florists' reel wire

1 m (1 yd) ribbon 15 mm (½ in–¾ in) wide

1 Take each bunch of herbs and sort them, making sure that the flowerheads are level. Then trim the stems to approximately 25 cm (10 in) long. Lay the herb bunches next to one another.

2 Hold the flowering mint in one hand and arrange the artemesia in a circle around the mint. Follow this with a circle of oregano, then marjoram and finally the sage.

3 Wind the wire round the posy three or four times and fasten it off securely. Trim the stems so that they are neat and even.

4 Cut 30 cm (12 in) of ribbon and tie it firmly round the stems to cover the wire. Leave two ribbon tails of similar length.

5 Make a double loop bow (see page 123) with the remaining 70 cm (28 in) of ribbon. Tie the bow in place using the ribbon tails and trim the ends at an angle for the final decorative flourish.

Informal bunches of herbs gathered together, tied with wire and finished with complementary tartan ribbon make the perfect gift for a friend's new kitchen.

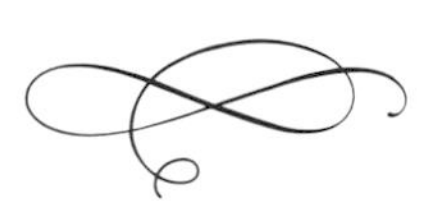

Pomanders

Scented pomanders and boules have been in existence for centuries. In the early days they were worn by noblemen and women as much to ward off disease as to make the wearer smell sweet. Now, these delightful objects are used to scent wardrobes and linen cupboards, bedrooms or china cabinets. Simple to make, the pomanders or boules – as I sometimes call these decorative spheres – in this chapter are an adaptation of their predecessors. Some are studded with roses, others are wrapped in soft moss or textured with graphic poppy seedheads. You can scent them with an essential oil or use them purely for ornamental purposes. Whatever you choose, you can be sure your guests will be unable to pass them by without an admiring comment.

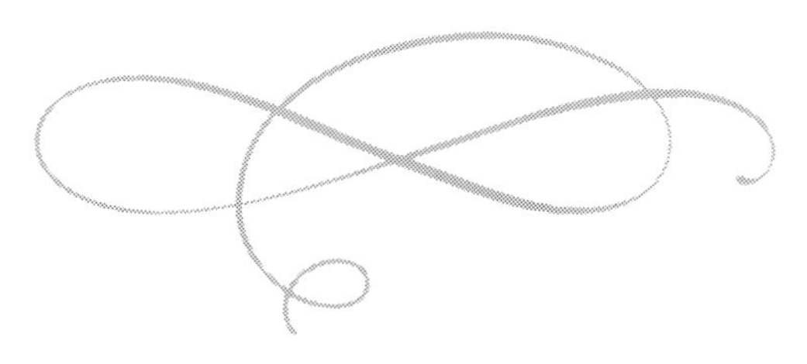

The way the house smells is an important factor as to how happy and relaxed I feel in my surroundings, and in my own home I have gently scented, aromatic pomanders and boules in most of the rooms. These mingle and blend to create a distinctive fragrance which I recognize as 'home' the minute I open my front door.

In my kitchen I have a little glass-fronted wall cupboard in which I store my herbs and spices and when I open the door I am enveloped in the most delicious mixture of aromatic fragrances.

A little way up the stairs is an antique housekeeper's cupboard which has a very old pomander in one of its compartments. Its faint, elusive scent creates a mood of nostalgia.

The making of pomanders has endured and evolved through the centuries from the time when silversmiths in Renaissance Venice first crafted elegant orbs to fill with *pomme d'ambre*, the apple-shaped balls of fragrant ambergris which were newly arrived from the East. These beautiful, decorative objects hung around the neck or from the waist and were believed to ward off disease as well as scent the wearer.

Clusters of flowers are tightly packed into a basic foam sphere to create these wonderful, textural pomanders.

The fashion of the pomander spread throughout Europe with holders being made from other precious materials such as gold, ivory and crystal. The pomander was in general use by the time of Elizabeth I of England, being worn by the nobility of the day. The silver pomander case of Mary Queen of Scots can still be seen by visitors to Holyrood House in Edinburgh.

Nowadays, there are generally two kinds of pomander available – the pierced china or silver receptacle for pot-pourri which is sold in shops; or the clove-studded orange that has been seasoned in an aromatic mixture of spices.

Try using roses you have grown and dried yourself as an economical way of completing these densely packed boules.

As the first requires no creative input at all, and the second requires far more time and patience than I generally have at my disposal, I have adapted the old ideas to new methods and materials and devised a contemporary equivalent of the *pomme d'ambre*.

Dry foam balls of various sizes are used as bases for the boules. Some are simply covered with moss, some with *Nigella orientalis* or safflowers, both of which are sturdy enough to be handled without damage. Others are studded with flowers like roses or *Helichrysum*.

When arranging a display of the boules I have found that odd numbers work far better than even numbers, so make up boules in threes, fives or sevens.

The sophisticated shapes, single colour and fresh scent of the boules makes them appropriate gifts for the most design conscious friend, regardless of whether they are male or female.

As with all the other projects in this book you should think of my ideas and interpretations as a starting point for your own imagination. Once you have mastered the techniques, don't limit yourself to the materials I have suggested, start to experiment and create your own designs. That's when the creativity really begins!

Green boules

The architectural quality of the sphere has appealed to me. Singly, they are objects of curiosity, and when grouped together, their different textures and variations in size create the possibility of a wide range of effects.

I have a large, shallow, wooden bowl of green boules on the coffee table in my sitting room. There is a tactile quality to these objects that is hard to resist and my visitors can seldom resist picking them up and turning them in their hands.

These boules can also be a highly decorative and attractive way to fragrance a room. In this instance, I prefer to use the citrus oils; lemon, grapefruit, bergamot, or a predominantly citrus-based blend, as these seem more appropriate than flowery oils.

If you wish to scent the boules, inject them with essential oils using a pipette. If you don't have a pipette, bore a hole into the ball with a skewer and drip the oil into the hole.

The single colour theme of these green boules emphasises their sculptural quality. As an alternative, rest them in the top of a terracotta pot or a small urn at either end of a mantelpiece.

MOSS BOULES

These moss boules are so simple to assemble; you can easily make five or six in an afternoon. Use plenty of pins to secure the moss, patching where necessary to achieve a good cover.

MATERIALS

7 cm (3 in) dry foam ball
9 cm (3½ in) dry foam ball
Dried sheet moss
Floral pins or stub wire bent into hairpin shapes
Citrus oil (optional)

1 Take one large and one small dry foam ball. Choose two pieces of moss that will generously wrap around each foam ball. (Overestimate the amount of moss rather than not allowing enough.)

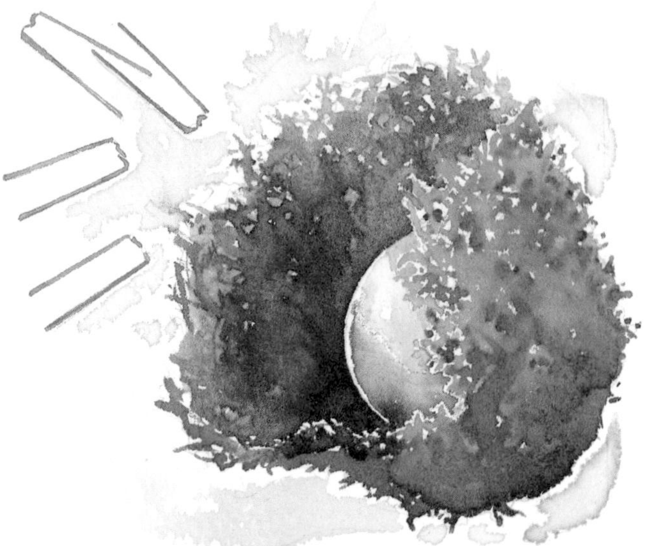

2 Place the foam ball in the middle of the moss and pin the moss to the foam using floral pins or bent stub wires. Gently tear off any excess moss and slightly overlap the edges.

3 The boules should look spherical, if there are any lumps or bumps, use more pins to correct the shape. If this does not work you may need to unwrap the moss and remove the excess.

NIGELLA BOULES

Spiky *Nigella orientalis* create a wonderful texture. Scent the foam first before adding the seedheads.

MATERIALS

7 cm (3 in) dry foam ball
9 cm (3½ in) dry foam ball
2 bunches of *Nigella orientalis*
Citrus oil (optional)

1 Cut the stems of the Nigella orientalis *seedheads to stems measuring approximately 4 cm (1½ in) long.*

2 Take one large and one small dry foam ball and push each seedhead firmly into the foam to cover the ball completely. Do this systematically; if you jump around you may end up with randomly spaced bald patches.

Soft green safflowers (left) and spiky Nigella orientalis *(right) create two exciting and unusual pomanders; they make appropriate gifts for the men in your life.*

SAFFLOWER BOULE

Safflowers – or *Carthamus* – have a complex shape which makes these boules so fascinating.

You may need to use gloves when working with safflowers as these can be slightly prickly.

MATERIALS

9 cm (3½ in) dry foam ball
1 bunch safflowers
Citrus oil (optional)

1 Cut the safflower flowerheads from the bunch to leave you with stems approximately 4 cm (1½ in) long.

2 Take one large dry foam ball and cover it methodically with flowerbuds until the whole surface is covered.

POPPY BOULE

A glue gun is a useful tool to create this boule. This pomander is a personal favourite; I think this boule looks like a highly decorative bomb!

MATERIALS

7 cm (3 in) dry foam ball
2 bunches poppy seedheads
Natural lichen
Hot glue
Citrus oil (optional)

1 Cut the poppy seedheads from the bunch, leaving you with stems approximately 4 cm (1½ in) long.

2 Place a blob of glue at the point where the seedhead meets the stem and then push the stem firmly into the foam.

3 Tuck some lichen round the base of each seedhead once it is in position. Repeat this process to cover the whole ball.

Flower boules

Whether displayed as a colourful group in a glass bowl or hung on a matching ribbon these pretty flower globes are eye-catching and appealing. Subtly scented with natural flower fragrances, I have found they make delightful air freshners. I have a group of three boules hanging at different levels in front of a little window in my cloakroom and they draw many admiring comments.

These boules also make delightful and stylish Christmas tree decorations. As well as the traditional tree, I have an antique terracotta pot filled with branches of twisted willow. Last year it was festooned with boules of red roses trimmed with gold voile bows.

I have used flowers in tones of red and yellows for this project: red roses, yellow dahlias, *Helichrysum* in shades of yellow and bronze, and yellow *Craspedia* and achillea. If the boules are destined for a traditional home, they will look their best if the colours used echo those of the room, if they are to be used in contemporary surroundings strongly contrasting colours are very exciting.

As roses are among the most expensive dried flowers, I dry my own using fresh roses bought from the market when they are at their most plentiful. The most economical way to buy roses for boules is to ask for packs of roseheads sold as ingredients for pot-pourri. They

Whether purely decorative or when scented for use as pomanders these flower boules are attractive gifts. Although all the boules in the picture have used a single colour theme, mixed colours can look beautiful – resembling Venetian glass paperweights.

are generally sold in mixed colours, but don't let this put you off, multi-coloured rose boules look very attractive. *Helichrysum* and dahlias are also sold without stems.

The achillea and *Craspedia* have strong stems which can simply be pushed into the foam ball, but as the roseheads, dahlias and *Helichrysum* have no stems, it is best to use a glue gun to fix the flowers to the foam ball.

Not all flowers are suitable, some are too fragile, and others are too expensive to use so intensively. Try mixing different flowers together, protecting delicate flowers with more robust companions or nestle valuable blooms in moss.

Delicately fragranced with flowery oils, and packed in tissue paper in a pretty box, these flower boules make ideal gifts for a favourite friend.

If you wish to scent the boules, inject them with essential oils using a pipette. If you don't have a pipette, bore a hole into the ball with a skewer and drip the oil into the hole.

ROSE BOULE

You can use this method to make a *Helichrysum* or dahlia boule. Remember to scent the ball before you begin attaching the flowers.

MATERIALS

For each boule you will need:
Approximately 50 roseheads
7 cm (3 in) dry foam ball
Essential rose oil (optional)
50 cm (20 in) of very narrow ribbon
Floral pin
Hot glue

1 *Make a loop with the ribbon and pin it on to the foam ball using the floral pin.*

2 *If the flowers have stems, cut them off close to the flowerhead. Using a glue gun, apply glue to the base of the flowerhead and hold each one firmly in place on the foam ball.*

3 *Cover the entire ball with flowers and then hang the completed boule by its loop while the hot glue sets.*

Craspedia *comes in a range of colours if you prefer a more colourful pomander.*

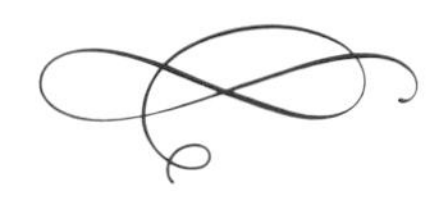

ACHILLEA & CRASPEDIA BOULE

Fabulous texture and warm colours; few can resist 'stroking' the round *Craspedia* flower-heads! If you want the boule to be scented, you must add the essential oil to the foam first.

MATERIALS

2 bunches *Craspedia* heads
1 bunch *Achillea filipendulina*
7 cm (3 in) dry foam ball
Scented oil of your choice (optional)
50 cm (20 in) of very narrow ribbon
Floral pin

1 *Make a loop with the ribbon and pin it on to the foam ball using the floral pin.*

2 *Trim the flower stems to 4 cm (1½ in) long. Starting next to the ribbon loop, push two or three* Craspedia *heads into the foam and then surround them with some* achillea *flowers.*

3 *Work your way around the foam ball, alternating groups of* Craspedia *with* achillea *until the boule is complete.*

Scented rose pomander

This pretty pomander is studded with tiny pink rosebuds and trimmed with a neat tartan ribbon. It has been scented with delicate tea rose oil to enhance the roses' natural fragrance.

The rosebuds used to make this pomander may seem to be the height of extravagance, but they are, in fact, sold quite inexpensively by botanical suppliers and herbalists.

A small dry foam ball is used as the base of the pomander. This is scented with a few drops of the tea rose oil before the pomander is made up. I use a glass pipette to inject the oil into the centre of the ball, but if you don't have one available, simply make a small hole with a skewer and drop the oil into the hole. It is best to put the oil into the centre of the ball as this slows down evaporation, and also prevents the oil from staining the ribbon. I generally prepare half a dozen balls at a time and then store them in a wooden box or tin until I want to use them. Do not store them in plastic as the oil leaches out.

Pure rose oils are prohibitively expensive and they are always diluted before being used, so any rose oil you buy will be mixed with another oil even if it doesn't say so on the label.

It is worth buying a good quality oil from a reputable supplier as it will have a higher amount of rose absolute in it than the cheaper ones. The cheapest oils are totally synthetic, with a harsh scent and poor lasting qualities.

Once the foam ball is well impregnated with oil, start work on the pomander. If you have very sensitive skin, I would recommend that you use fine rubber gloves, as both the foam and the oils can cause skin irritation. Also avoid touching your eyes when you work with these materials.

Conveniently the rosebuds come with little stalks which push home neatly into the foam. If the pomander is unlikely to be handled much you will not need to use glue, but if you want to be quite certain that the rosebuds will not work loose, you can dip each stalk into an all-purpose glue before pushing them into the foam.

This is an ideal project where children can help and results in a perfect present for teacher.

MATERIALS

For each pomander you will need:
7 cm (3 in) diameter dry foam ball
60 g (2 oz) rosebuds
1.5 m (1¾ yd) of 15 mm (½ in) wide ribbon
Pins
Tea rose oil
All-purpose glue (optional)

1 Using a pipette, inject the foam ball with tea rose oil. Alternatively, make a hole in the ball with a skewer and drip the oil into the centre of the foam. Ideally leave the ball to 'cure' for a few days.

2 Cut the ribbon into two pieces – one roughly 85 cm (34 in) long and the other around 65 cm (26 in) long. Pin the shorter piece of ribbon around the ball and secure it with a knot. Leave the tails hanging loose.

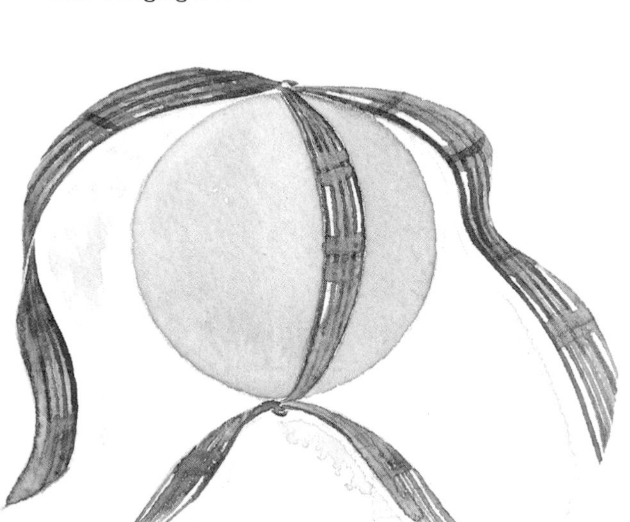

3 Now pin the longer piece of ribbon round the ball at right angles to the first. Fasten it at the same point as the first ribbon and use the hanging tails to make a neat bow to cover the knots.

4 Tie the tails from the second piece of ribbon together to make the loop by which to hang the pomander. Remove any visible pins.

5 Finally, stud the four quadrants with rosebuds, first dipping them into glue, if you wish, and making sure that you pack them closely together to avoid any foam showing.

Pink rosebuds stud a scented foam ball to make a rose pomander. The burgundy and green tartan ribbon quarters the pomander and is used to make a loop to hang it by. A red rosebud pomander looks equally good with a gold brocade ribbon.

Terracotta pots

The warm, natural earth tones of terracotta are a perfect foil for dried flower arrangements. As the subtle blooms are a muted reminder of the fresh flowers of summer, so the terracotta is a gentle echo of the soil in which they grew. So many flowers, grasses, mosses and leaves of varying shapes and hues sit well in an old weathered pot: roses, sunflowers and wheat are just some examples you can use. Or try a popular design where an ivory-coloured candle is potted amidst flowers and moss.

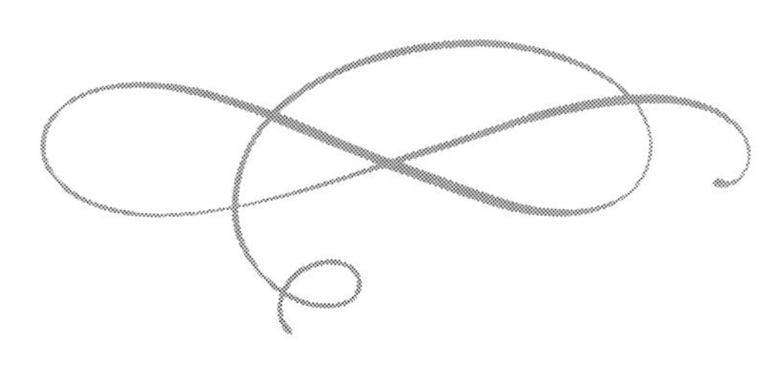

For many years I lived on a farm where stacked outside the potting shed were the wonderful old pots that had been used since Victorian times. Modern methods meant that plastic pots were generally used for growing plants, so I was fortunate to have a wonderful source of beautifully aged and weathered containers for my dried flowers. I still have some left, but I also keep a keen look out in country junk shops and market stalls so that I can replenish my ever-dwindling supplies.

Old, weathered terracotta is often pitted and, because the pots were made by hand, they have slightly misshapen sides which adds to their charm. Surprisingly, old terracotta, if treated with care, can last just as long as new – it does tend to be a little more brittle owing to its age and condition. However, many people prefer to buy clean, new terracotta pots. Some are decorated with patterns and scalloped edges and you can, of course, choose this modern, more ornate terracotta for your designs.

Use small flowers to outline, emphasise and link larger flowers like these peonies surrounded by tiny roses, asters and pink achillea. Moss disguises the edge of the pot and softens the meeting point between the flowers and the terracotta.

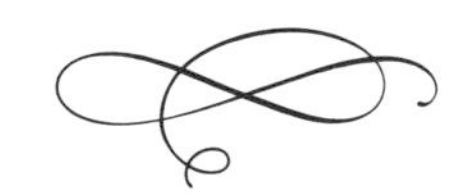

If you like the look of old terracotta but can only find new pots, try distressing the surface of the pot to give it the appearance of age. Paint the terracotta with natural yoghurt and then leave it outside for several weeks to grow moss and lichen. If you are in real hurry, try rubbing the surface with a cream cleanser used for cleaning kitchens and bathrooms. Apply either the yoghurt or the cleanser in a random fashion, so that the pot looks fairly rugged. While these methods are a good compromise; only time will really give a pot that authentic, weathered look and soften the colour of the warm orange.

Virtually any dried flower combination sits well in terracotta; although roses and moss seem to be a most admirable mix. In this chapter, I have used roses for two of the projects: in miniature terracotta pots known as 'tiny toms', and to decorate the candle pot.

A series of scented pots is another variation on a pot display. Here, tightly packed blooms fill the pot and spill over the sides, each pot emiting a beautiful fragrance to complement the flowers.

Perhaps one of the most unusual and challenging designs is the hellebore pot. Unlike ordinary dried flowers, I have waxed these spectacular blooms so that they look almost fresh. This method of flower preservation was often used by the Victorians, and I have explained how satisfying it is to employ today.

Whichever project you select, remember that the terracotta pot is a sympathetic vehicle for dried flowers which will complement all sorts of interpretations.

Wonderful textures and soft pastels are created by this mixture of achillea, *peonies and* roses.

Victorian rose pot

A few years ago, the plant nurseries at Windsor Castle were modernised and a friend of mine bought all the old terracotta pots. Among the orchid pots, seed pans and long toms were some minute, delightfully named 'tiny toms'. The scale of these pots was so small that I decided to do something very simple that would not detract from the beauty of these miniature pots. The Victorian Rose Pot could not be simpler to make and, while desirable, a pot with royal connections is not essential!

The pot is filled with dry foam which has been scented with tea rose oil and then covered with tumbling sheet moss and three dark red rose-heads are then arranged on the cushion of moss.

These little pots make lovely individual presents and look marvellous when used as table decorations next to each place setting, or when grouped informally on a mantelpiece.

Tiny terracotta flowerpots only need some artfully arranged moss and rosebuds to make an arrangement. With the addition of wire cardholders they can be used as novel place markers.

1 Using a long-bladed knife, cut the foam block to fit the pot so that it stands slightly proud of the top of the pot.

2 If you wish to scent the arrangement, now is the time to do so. Very carefully, add five drops of perfume oil to the foam. (The oil can affect sensitive skin, so wear gloves to protect your hands.)

MATERIALS

5 cm (2 in) diameter terracotta pot
Dry foam block
Dried sheet moss
3 roses
Floral pin or stub wire
Tea rose oil (optional)
Hot glue

3 Flatten out the moss and arrange it over the foam. Use a floral pin or stub wire bent into a hairpin shape to pin the moss into place. Ensure that the moss falls over the edge of the pot.
If the piece of moss is too large, tear pieces off rather than cutting it, as this gives it a softer edge. Fasten the moss to the pot with hot glue from a glue gun.

4 Trim the rose stems to around 5 cm (2 in) and, if necessary, apply some steam to the roseheads to give you fuller flowers. (See page 120 for instructions on how to do this.)

5 Apply glue to the base of the flowerheads and push the stems through the moss so that the roseheads rest on top.

Sunflower pot

The sunflower pot is a homage to Van Gogh. I seldom leave the stems of the flowers showing in the way they do in this arrangement, but in this case it seems quite appropriate. The simplicity of this pot is very appealing and it is best displayed in uncluttered surroundings where it looks wonderful against natural brick or aged wood.

MATERIALS

15 cm (6 in) diameter terracotta pot
Dry foam block
Sunflowers
Dry sheet moss
Floral pins or stub wire

Sunflowers do not require sophisticated treatment. An old terracotta pot is a sympathetic container for this rustic arrangement which looks perfectly at home on a painted pine shelf. Sunflowers look their best in rough textured containers – try them in a coarse woven basket, an old galvanized watering can or a wooden trug.

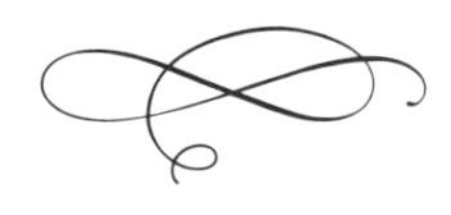

1 Using a long-bladed knife, cut the foam block so that it can be squeezed into the flower pot. The foam should be level with the top of the pot. Trim it with the knife if necessary.

2 Cover the top of the pot with the moss and pin in place using floral pins or stub wire bent into hair pin shapes.

3 Begin inserting the sunflowers, placing the central flower first. The length of the flower stem above the moss should be approximately the same as the height of the pot. Working from the central flower outwards, add further flowers, gradually shortening the stems as you work towards the outside edge of the pot, until the pot is full.

Wheatsheaf

This design has a classical formality that belies its rustic roots. In this instance, I have added lightly gilded salal leaves. If you cannot get salal substitute holly oak. The soft green of the leaves is exactly the same colour as the wheat stems and the gilding echoes the gold voile ribbon. To gild the leaves I have rubbed them with a gilt wax which is generally used for picture frames. You can buy gilt wax from art supply shops: it is usually sold in little pots. The effect of gilt wax is much softer than spray paint and more controllable. A pair of wheatsheaf pots, one at either end of a mantelpiece, adds sophistication.

Wheatsheaves have been used for decoration since classical times. Their association with harvest and fertility would make a pair of wheatsheaf pots an ideal decorative and symbolic wedding present.

MATERIALS

For each pot you will need:
10 cm (4 in) diameter terracotta pot
Bunch wheat
3 stems salal or holly oak leaves
Dried sheet moss
1.5 m (1¾ yd) × 40 mm (1½ in) wide gold voile ribbon
Dry foam block
Garden string or raffia
Gilt wax

1 *If you buy the wheat in a bundle, untie it first. Then place the wheat, head first, in a wide-necked vase or bucket. This is an easy way to ensure that the heads are level.*

2 *Lift the wheat bundle out and spend a few minutes arranging any straggling stems. Bind the bundle firmly with string or raffia, 5 cm (2 in) below the ears of wheat.*

3 Using the tip of your finger, rub a little gilt wax on to the leaves. Arrange the leaves around the wheat ears and bind them in place with more string or raffia.

4 Bind the stems again 25 cm (10 in) below the ears of wheat. Now trim the stems level so that the wheatsheaf is 40 cm (16 in) long.

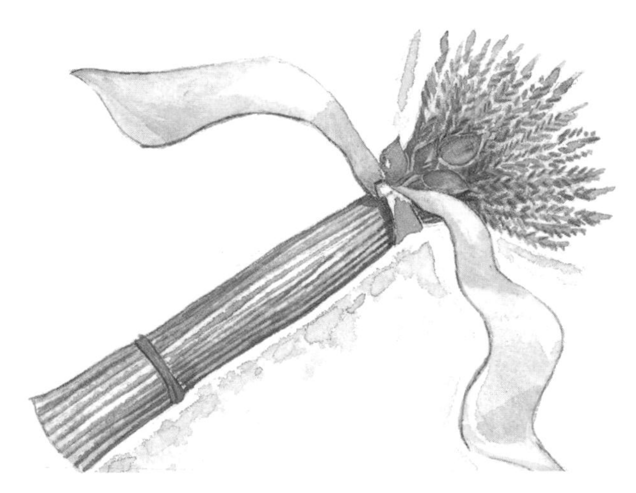

5 Cut the ribbon in half and tie one 75 cm (30 in) length around the upper binding, leaving the tails hanging loose.

6 Make a double bow from the other 75 cm (30 in) length of ribbon (see page 123 on how to make bows) and tie it to the wheatsheaf using the tails from the first piece of ribbon.

7 Stand the wheatsheaf upright in the pot and support it with wedges of foam. Arrange the moss over the foam and glue it in place.

Scented flowerpots

Scented flowerpots are one of the prettiest ways I know to add fragrance to a room. I love the way the flowers hug the pot and cascade over the sides. As with most dried flower arrangements, the secret of their success lies in keeping the stems of the flowers really short and packing them tightly together so that the final effect is of a densely packed flower border. I like to make a few pots at a time and experiment with different colour combinations, textures and shapes.

When using large flowers, such as peonies or *Achillea filipendulina* heads, I am careful not to place one of these flowers centrally in the pot, as this spoils the informality of the design and makes it difficult to achieve a balanced arrangement. Similarly, you will see that I generally group small flowers together rather than use them individually as they have more impact this way and it avoids the 'bitty' look that is sometimes present in arrangements.

As each pot is relatively economical with the flowers it uses, I can use up all the half bunches that have been left over from larger projects.

I like to use a perfume oil that is sympathetic to the flowers, for example, a citrus oil seemed appropriate for the bright yellow and orange arrangement, while the pinks and blues of the pot filled with peonies, asters and roses has been fragranced with a blend of oils called Summer Garden. There are many pot-pourri refresher oils available these days and they are ideal for scented arrangements. If you are giving your scented flowerpots as gifts, it is a nice touch to give the recipient a phial of the perfume oil, so that they can renew the fragrance as it fades.

Save your home-dried blooms for these small scale arrangements. Moss roses, astrantia, alchemilla are all suitable and seldom available in the shops.

MATERIALS

For each pot you will need:
10 cm (4 in) diameter terracotta pot
Dried sheet moss
A selection of flowers
Dry foam block
Perfume oil of your choice
Hot or all-purpose glue

1 Using a long-bladed knife, cut the foam to fit the pot, allowing about 3 cm (1 in) of foam to stand proud of the pot rim. Squeeze the foam into the pot and then trim edges with the knife so that the foam slopes down to the rim of the pot. Fragrance the foam with five drops of your chosen oil.

2 Glue the moss in place over the foam ensuring that it falls over the edge of the pot in a naturalistic way.

3 Trim the stems of the flowers to about 5 cm (2 in) long. Start your arrangement with a large flower positioned off centre and then build your design around that flower.

4 As you work, look at the pot from the side as well as from above to ensure that you keep the outline regular. Angle the stems inwards as you position the flowers towards the edge of the pot so that the line of flowers continues over the rim.

Scented flowerpots make perfect presents. The bright yellows and reds of the pot at the top of the picture are enhanced with a zingy citrus fragrance, and would look good in a modern setting, while the soft pinks and yellows of the lower pot, complemented by a gentle tea rose fragrance, are ideal for a traditionally decorated bedroom.

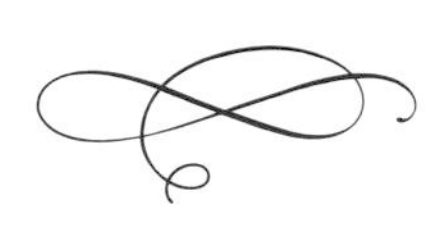

Candle pot

Peppercorns, bay leaves and roses garland this Candle pot. If you have difficulty obtaining the pink peppercorns, you could use some of the realistic fake berries.

Dried flowers and candles complement one another wonderfully well, but it must be recognised that the combination is a potential fire risk. It is important that any arrangement is constructed in such a way that the risk is minimised and that the candles are *never* left burning unattended.

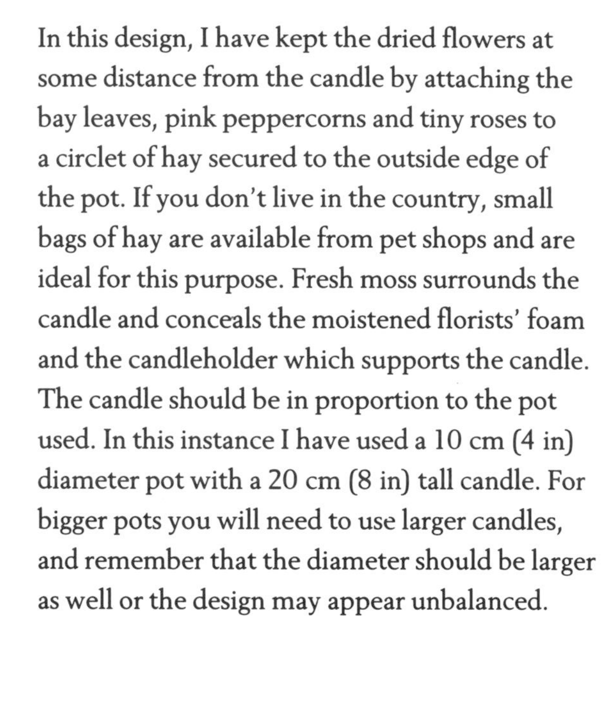

In this design, I have kept the dried flowers at some distance from the candle by attaching the bay leaves, pink peppercorns and tiny roses to a circlet of hay secured to the outside edge of the pot. If you don't live in the country, small bags of hay are available from pet shops and are ideal for this purpose. Fresh moss surrounds the candle and conceals the moistened florists' foam and the candleholder which supports the candle. The candle should be in proportion to the pot used. In this instance I have used a 10 cm (4 in) diameter pot with a 20 cm (8 in) tall candle. For bigger pots you will need to use larger candles, and remember that the diameter should be larger as well or the design may appear unbalanced.

MATERIALS

10 cm (4 in) diameter terracotta pot
4 bay leaves
20 tiny roseheads
4 bunches pink peppercorns
Hay
Fine florists' wire
Foam for fresh flowers
20 cm (8 in) tall candle
Candleholder
Small plastic bag
Fresh moss
Hot glue

1 Line the pot with the plastic bag. Using a long-bladed knife, cut the foam so that it fits inside the pot, ensuring that the foam sits 4 cm (1½ in) below the rim of the pot. Trim the plastic bag just above the level of the foam. Push the candleholder into the centre of the foam.

2 Take a generous handful of hay and pull it out into a sausage shape. Starting at one end, wrap the florists' wire round and round to form a rope of hay.

3 Check the circumference of the pot and make the circle of hay slightly smaller than the top edge of the pot. Push the circlet of hay in place from below, and once you are satisfied that it fits snugly, glue it in place.

4 Glue the leaves, peppercorns and roses in place. If the leaves are brittle, hold them over some steam before you glue them in position. Insert the candle into the holder and surround it with fresh moss. Moisten the foam before lighting the candle and replace the moss when it fades.

Hellebore pot

Waxing flowers was extremely popular in Victorian times, but is little practised these days. In its heyday, no Victorian parlour was complete without an elaborate arrangement of waxed flowers under a glass dome. This is far too funereal for modern tastes, but I wanted to experiment with the process to see if I could come up with a contemporary interpretation.

Using a technique that was very popular in Victorian times, these hellebores have been dried and then waxed. This method allows them to be arranged in a very naturalistic style so that the flowers appear to be growing amongst the twigs in an old terracotta pot. This method can also be used on daffodils, snowdrops and tulips.

I used hellebore flowers for two reasons. First, it was the middle of winter when I first read about waxing flowers, and hellebores were the only remotely suitable flowers blooming in my garden; and secondly, they are among my favourite flowers and I wanted to see if I could successfully capture their beauty.

It worked wonderfully well, and while the flowers do start to fade after three months or so, it is a fascinating way to preserve these delicate flowers and enjoy their beauty indoors.

I have since used the technique successfully on other flowers and have found that it is best to use flowers that already have a natural waxy coating on their petals. Most of the spring flowers are suitable, daffodils, narcissus, tulips and hyacinths, and it also works well with lilies, camellias and gardenias.

You will need more equipment and materials than usual for this project, but as both the wax and the dessicant are re-usable you will be able to repeat the process many times.

The stems of the hellebore are quite fleshy, so I strengthen them with wire, before drying the flowers in dessicant (see page 119 for more details on how to do this). Once the flowers are sufficiently dry (4–7 days), I carefully remove them from the dessicant and paint them with melted paraffin wax. Paraffin wax is available from chemists. It has a very low melting point, so there is no danger of burning yourself; in fact it is positively good for the skin and once you have finished waxing the flowers you can give your hands a beauty treatment by dipping them in wax.

The finished flowers are quite delicate so I have given them some protection by arranging them among silver birch twigs. Hellebores grow happily in shady gardens so this is a naturalistic setting for the flowers, and as a finishing touch I have encircled the pot with silver birch twigs.

Silver birch trees drop lengths of twig in strong winds so there is no need to pick them from the living tree. I usually pick up a few stems when I walk in the woods and have even been known to stop my car to gather up some particularly fine pieces from the pavement. I keep a bundle of the twigs under a bush in my garden where they stay moist and pliable.

The hellebore pot is a real conversation piece, and, with the addition of some fine taper candles it makes a wonderful centrepiece for a table.

MATERIALS

10 cm (4 in) diameter terracotta pot
3–5 stems hellebore flowers
2 kg (5 lb) dessicant
Plastic box or biscuit tin
Stub wire
500 g (1 lb) paraffin wax
Paintbrush
Dry foam block
Silver birch twigs
Dry moss
Hot or all-purpose glue

1 *Very carefully insert a stub wire up the stem of the hellebore. Feed the wire in slowly, holding the stem so that you can control the direction of the wire. Trim the end of the wire level with the stem.*

2 *Lay the flowers in the dessicant (see page 119) and leave the flowers to dry. Check after 4 days; if the stems are dry the flowers are ready for use, if not leave them, checking every other day until they are ready. Pour the dessicant from the container and remove the flowers.*

3 *Use half the block of foam as a stand for the flowers. Put the paraffin wax into a small metal or plastic bowl and place this in a pan of hot water so that the wax melts.*

4 *Hold one stem at a time over the bowl and gently brush on the paraffin wax. It is best to apply the wax fairly sparingly or you may end up with more wax than flower. Coat the stems as well and return the flowers to the foam stand.*

Twigs help to support the waxed heads of the hellebores as well as providing them with a decorative setting. The soft sheen of the wax coating adds lustre.

5 Take a length of silver birch twig about 75 cm (30 in) long and twist it round on itself to make a circlet slightly smaller than the circumference of the upper rim of the flowerpot.

6 Push the circlet in place round the pot. It should fit snugly just below the rim. Fasten it in place using a few spots of glue.

7 Using a long-bladed knife, cut the foam to fit into the pot, so that it finishes just below the rim. Cover the foam with moss.

8 Finally, arrange the hellebore flowers in the pot, interspersing them with silver birch twigs which should be slightly taller in size than the hellebores themselves.

Topiary trees

These elegant and stylish trees are not as difficult to make as you might think. Conical or mop-head shapes, tall or short, these delightful objets d'art make wonderful gifts or are satisfying to keep for yourself to adorn your own mantelpiece. Some of the trees in this chapter are made from foam shapes which are covered with moss, but there is no reason why you cannot adapt the designs shown here to make trees of bold seedheads or dense flowerheads.

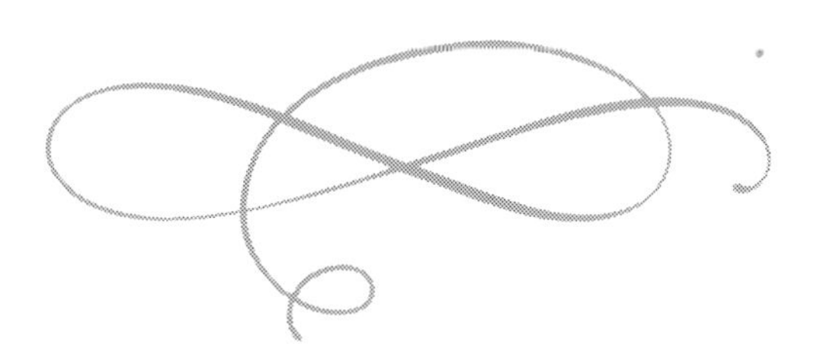

Moss topiary

You need never be stuck for a gift to please and impress your friends once you realise how easy it is to make these moss trees. Twigs, dry florists' foam, moss, a pot plus a few mechanics are all you need to begin.

I recently taught a workshop at The Chelsea Physic Garden in London where 40 students made topiary trees. As they worked they were seated at two long tables on either side of the room and when they had completed the project the effect of the two lines of trees was stunning. All we needed was a miniature stately home at the end of the avenue to complete the illusion!

In the past, these elegant trees have been the exclusive province of the designer florists, but now that the materials are relatively easy to obtain, there is no reason why you cannot make your own trees for a fraction of the cost. Topiary trees are extremely simple to assemble and are fashionable decorative accessories which will look at home in most contemporary surroundings.

Like living topiary, this moss topiary is most effective when grouped together. This dramatic setting illustrates the successful combination of statuary and topiary.

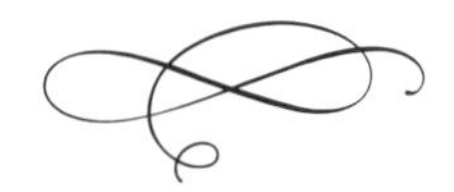

The moss is pinned on to dry foam cones or balls to form the topiary shape and the trunks of the trees are formed from wired bundles of twigs. I have used an old terracotta pot as my container. To ensure that the tree stands firmly I have lined the pot with foam and then set the trunk in plaster of Paris. It is important to line the pot as the plaster expands and generates heat as it sets and will crack the container if the pot is unlined. You can, if you wish, use something grander than a terracotta pot; for instance a china cache pot or a small urn, but if you do so I would recommend that you make your tree in a plastic pot which can then be slipped inside the decorative one.

It is important to achieve the correct proportions when making these trees, and a general rule of thumb is that the circumference of the dry foam ball or the base of the cone should be approximately the same as the rim of the pot you intend using. It does not matter if it is slightly smaller as the moss will increase its size, but be careful that it is not much larger or your tree will look top-heavy.

With the short drumhead tree the visible length of the trunk should be roughly the same as the height of the pot, and one-and-a-half times the height of the pot for the tall drumhead tree. When you are making a conifer tree, be careful to have a short length of trunk showing or your tree will end up looking like a gnome's hat!

These rules apply whatever the size of your topiary tree.

TALL DRUMHEAD TREE

These standard mop-head trees look very effective, especially in pairs or small groups. Once you have made one, you might well be encouraged to make several more!

MATERIALS

10 cm (4 in) diameter pot
9 cm (3½ in) dry foam ball
Dried sheet moss
Bundle 30 cm (12 in) long twigs
Floral pins or stub wire
Dry foam block
Plaster of Paris
Fine florists' wire
Hot glue

1 To make the trunk, wire together both ends of the bundle of twigs. Pull the wire tightly so that the twigs are neat and secure.

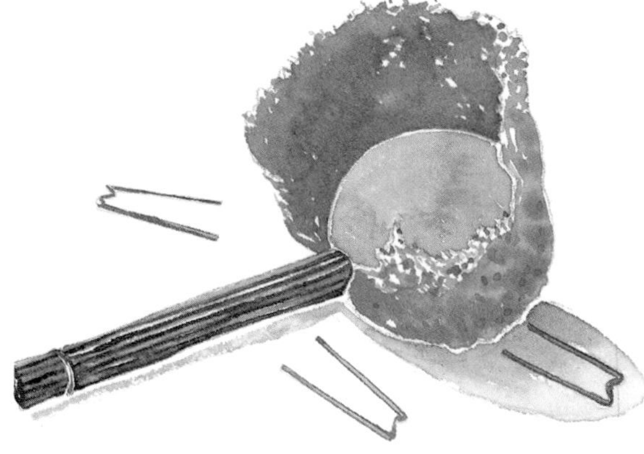

2 Push one end of the trunk firmly into the foam ball and remove it immediately. Put a generous amount of glue into the hole you have made and replace the trunk. Set it aside for the glue to dry thoroughly.

3 Choose a piece of moss that will wrap generously around the foam ball. Place the foam ball in the middle of the moss and pin the moss to the foam using floral pins or stub wires. Gently tear off any excess moss and slightly overlap the edges before pinning it finally in place.

4 The drumhead should look spherical, if there are any lumps or bumps use more pins to correct the shape. If this does not work you may need to unwrap the moss and remove any excess. It is worth taking a bit of time to get the shape right.

5 Now cut a piece of foam to fit the pot, using a long-bladed knife. Make a well in the centre of the foam by pushing a cylindrical object, like a candle, into the foam. You want to create a hole which is roughly 5 cm (2 in) wide and 6 cm (2½ in) deep.

6 Mix up plaster of Paris to a thick paste with water and half fill hole. Stand the prepared tree upright in the plaster and leave it to set. It does not take long to firm up, but you need to leave it for several hours for it to set really hard. Finish by covering the foam and plaster with moss.

Variations

SHORT DRUMHEAD TREE

This is made in exactly the same way as the first tree, except that you will need 25 cm (10 in) twigs to make a shorter trunk.

CONIFER TREE

When making the conifer tree you will need a series of 20 cm (8 in) twigs to form the trunk.

Lay the foam cone on its side on the moss and pin the moss to the cone in a straight line from top to bottom, and then roll the moss round the cone pinning as you go and gently tearing away the excess. Fold the moss under the base of the cone and pin it in place around the trunk.

Topiary trees are very easy to make and visually pleasing. Sheet moss has been pinned on to foam balls and cones to make the heads of the trees and the stems have been made from bundles of twigs. Alternatively moss or lichen covered branches make highly decorative tree trunks.

Twisted willow tree

Purists may feel that adding any decoration to twisted willow branches is gilding the lily, but I could not resist combining them with some flower boules to create this unusual design. The combination of rosebuds and *Nigella* seedheads works well together and the effect is similar to large artichoke heads just coming into bloom.

The twisted willow branches are supported by a block of foam which has been set in plaster of Paris inside a plastic pot. The plastic pot is then slipped into the terracotta pot and the plaster is disguised with sheet moss.

Once the branches are firmly fixed I trim them where necessary to achieve a balanced shape. Before decorating the foam balls, I decide on their position and push them in place on the chosen branches, again shortening or cutting away branches until I am happy with the design. I have used two different size balls for added interest. These are then removed from the branches and decorated with the rosebuds and *Nigella* before being glued back in position.

This design may not appeal to traditionalists, but for those with a taste for the unusual this makes a highly original gift.

MATERIALS

3 × 60 cm (20 in) willow branches
13 cm (5 in) diameter terracotta pot
10 cm (4 in) plastic pot
Dry foam block
2 × 9 cm (3½ in) diameter foam balls
7 cm (3 in) diameter foam ball
60 g (2 oz) rosebuds
2 bunches *Nigella orientalis*
Sheet moss
Plaster of Paris
Hot glue

The contorted shapes of twisted willow inspired this design. The 'artichoke flowers' are made from balls of foam studded with Nigella orientalis *and rosebuds. Alternatively, for a minimalist effect, moss-covered globes give a stark simplicity.*

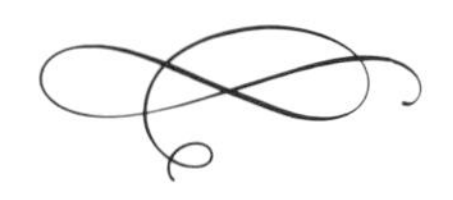

1 Using a long-bladed knife, cut the foam so that it fits loosely in the plastic pot.

2 Arrange the branches in the foam to create a good outline. Trim or cut away any branches that spoil the shape.

3 Mix the plaster of Paris to a thick paste with water and fill the pot so that the plaster comes to within 1 cm (1/2 in) from the rim.

4 Slip the plastic pot into the terracotta pot and cover the surface with sheet moss.

5 Position the dry foam balls on the twisted willow branches, trimming the ends of the branches to ensure a clean fit.

6 Remove the balls and, starting directly opposite the hole in the foam, make a star pattern with the rosebuds, pushing them firmly into the foam. This should cover roughly a third of the ball.

7 Trim the Nigella orientalis, *leaving stalks 4 cm (1 1/2 in) long. Cover the rest of the ball with* Nigella *heads. Put a generous amount of glue into the hole in the foam ball and push the completed 'flower' on to the twisted willow.*

There is something celebratory about a garland. It doesn't need a practical function, for its chief purpose is to beautify its surroundings and give us pleasure. I love to walk around a city at Christmas time admiring all the festive garlands on the doors, and it pleases me that so many people still have time for celebration in their busy lives. While Christmas is undoubtedly the time of year when garlands are most popular, they do make wonderful room decorations throughout the seasons.

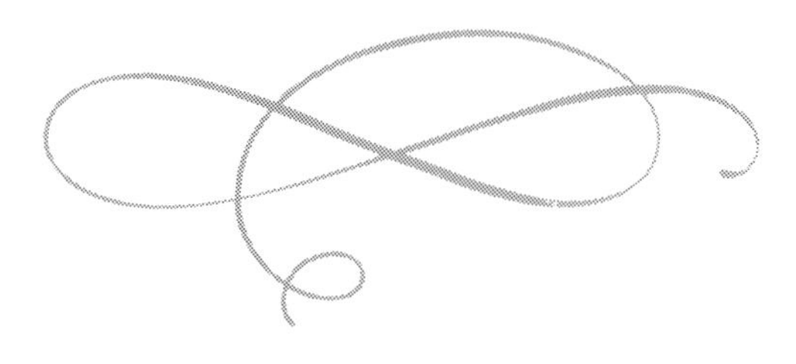

Below: The flat matt colours of the olive wood wreath, the pine cones and the bark are brought to life by the gilded twigs and mushrooms and a last minute addition of fresh tendrils of ivy

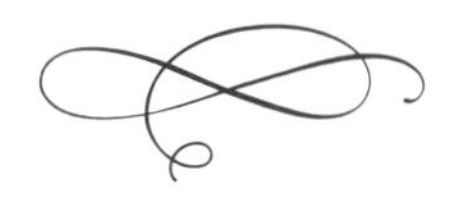

Although there is sometimes a problem finding table space for a dried flower arrangement, there is nearly always room on a wall for a garland. One of my favourite spots for displaying garlands is above the doorway to a room. It is out of harm's way and adds interest to a space frequently left unadorned.

Nowadays, it is possible to buy many types of undecorated garlands from shops and garden centres and most of them can be used as bases for dried flower designs. In my workroom I have garlands made from straw, vines, olive wood, lavender stems and even roots and fern leaves, all of which I use for my designs, and it is good to know that many of these materials are from renewable resources which were unused in the past and now provide work and income for third-world villagers.

All my designs use simple techniques, and I generally avoid anything that involves a great deal of fiddly wiring of flowers or other time-consuming procedures. This is particularly true with gar-

lands where I use a glue gun or floral pins for most of the work.

When adding strong focal points on garlands, such as bows or large flowers, you may find it easier to achieve a balanced design if you use odd numbers – 3, 5, or 7. With even numbers the focal points must be symmetrical or the design won't work.

Once you have mastered the basic techniques you too will be able to make your own designs and fill your home with glorious garlands.

Above: Silvery sage and artemesia *blend with the soft greens of bay and marjoram and the purple oregano to create a bouquet garni on a grand scale. Left: Luscious Bowl of Beauty peonies with frilly cream stamens set around with bunches of lavender and sprays of deep pink roses are dramatic focal points on the summer garland.*

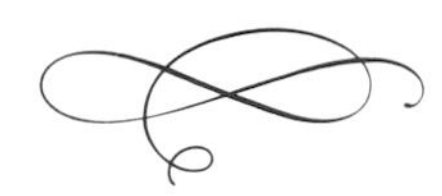

Moss ring

Of all the bases I use, I find the straw wreath the most useful. When I first worked with dried flowers I used preformed foam rings to make my garlands, and although it was extremely easy to glue the flowers in place, I wasn't happy with the results, especially as the foam was fragile and did not support some of the weightier flowers I like to use. I have found the straw ring ideal, it is strong and well-proportioned and fixing the moss and flowers to it could not be easier.

Sometimes, simple lines are the most pleasing. This plain moss wreath echoes the purity of its surroundings and enhances the textures around it. Try adding some seashells and driftwood to give this garland a nautical air.

Before you decorate any garland, it is essential to attach the ring by which to hang the garland. This may sound obvious, but I am sure that I am not the only person to have completed a design only to discover that I have omitted this step and that what should have been a simple procedure becomes extremely fiddly as I attempt to fasten the ring securely without damaging the flowers. I use small brass or plastic rings which are sold for ruched blinds and are available from most haberdashery departments.

When the mood takes me, I prepare a number of moss garlands which can be stored until I need them. The moss provides a perfect background for many of my designs, two of which are projects in this chapter.

In an ideal world, moss would always come in large, flat sheets of a consistent thickness. Instead, it is rather like my pastry, sometimes it co-operates and at other times it's made up of lots of odd-shaped bits that have to be patched together. Don't fret if this happens to you; as long as you don't skimp on the floral pins or stub wires, any size moss will do the job.

MATERIALS

30 cm (12 in) diameter straw wreath
Sheet moss
Floral pins or stub wires
Reel wire
Brass or plastic ring

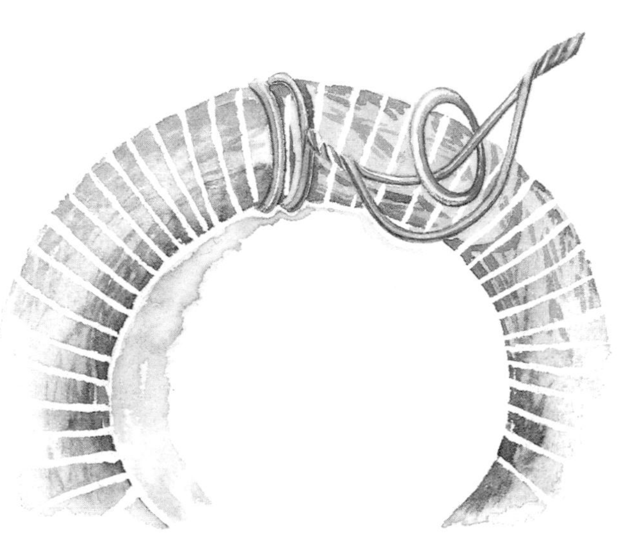

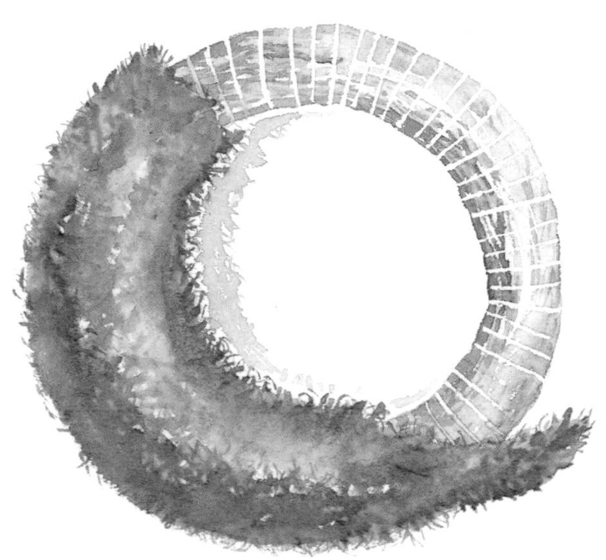

1 Wrap the reel wire around the wreath a couple of times and then thread the brass or plastic ring on to the wire and fasten it off securely. Tie a piece of string to the ring so that you do not lose it among the moss.

2 Cover the entire ring with the moss, pinning it securely in place with the floral pins or stub wires. Where it is necessary to remove excess moss, tear it rather than cutting it to avoid obvious joins.

3 Store completed moss rings in plastic bags or minimalists may be perfectly happy to display them as they are.

Summer garland

Nowadays, many of the flowers of summer are available all year round in the modern florist's shop. With blooms air-freighted around the world and hot-house technology extending the growing season, we happily accept flowers out of season. Tulips in autumn and delphiniums and snapdragons in the middle of winter are no longer a surprise.

MATERIALS

Prepared moss ring (see page 80)
6 peony flowers
Bunch lavender
Bunch bright pink tiny roses
Floral pins or stub wire
Reel wire
Hot glue

The hot pinks of the Bowl of Beauty peonies and little roses, combined with the deep blue lavender, remind us of warm summer days in this colourful garland. By using contrasting rather than complementary colours you can create a dazzling effect. Bright yellow achillea or sunflowers would also look stunning with the lavender.

One of the flowers that has thus avoided this fate is the peony, that most glorious and transient of summer flowers, and this makes it a particularly desirable dried flower.

I have some wonderful peony plants in my garden, but I cannot bear to cut the flowers for drying, so each year I make a pilgrimage to a grower where I buy large quantities of these gorgeous blooms. The scent of the flowers *en masse* is quite wonderful, spicy and lemony and not at all heavy. I consider burying my face in an armful of full-blown peonies to be one of life's great experiences. Once home I hang the peonies upside down above my range to dry where they look like rows of ballerinas' tutus. (For full details of how to dry peonies see page 118.)

The peony most often used commercially for drying is the pale pink Sarah Bernhardt, but for this garland I have used the stunning Bowl of Beauty, with its large, deep-pink petals surrounding a mass of smaller ivory petals. The peonies are set among sprays of matching little spray roses and bunches of deep blue lavender in a garland that pays tribute to the hot colours and heady scents of high summer.

1 *Place the prepared moss ring on the table with the hanging ring face down directly opposite you. This will mark the top of the garland and you can arrange your flowers around this focal point.*

2 *Divide the lavender into 6 small bunches, bind each with wire and trim the stalks to 15 cm (6 in) long.*

3 Arrange the lavender bunches on the garland, with three on each side pointing towards the top. The stems of the bottom two bunches should cross. Fasten these with floral pins or stub wire.

4 Place one peony head in the centre at the top and one in the centre at the bottom and glue these in place.

5 Arrange the remaining four peonies over the lavender bunches on either side of the garland and glue them in place so that they conceal the pins.

6 Pin individual sprigs of roses around the lavender and peonies, not forgetting the inner and outer edges of the ring.

The glorious yellow centres of these Bowl of Beauty peonies are a wonderful example of the fabulous contrasts in nature.

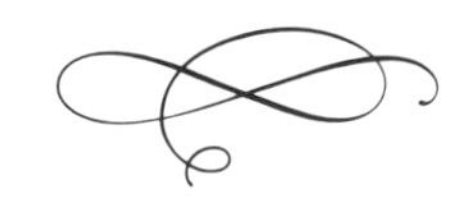

Christmas wreath

The wreath that we hang on our door at Christmas time first became popular in the United States and was an adaptation of the Advent Wreath that the Scandinavians took to the New World. Like many other traditions that we now consider integral to Christmas, the Advent Wreath had its origins in pagan times with the Norse candlelight ceremonies for the darkest days of the year. Originally, the wreath would be a simple circle of evergreens but nowadays, you will find garlands made from every imaginable natural and artificial material, from pine cones to ruched ribbon.

MATERIALS

50 cm (20 in) diameter olive wood or similar wreath
25 pine cones
4 × 5 cm (2 in) diameter flower pots
Golden mushrooms
Sheet moss
Dry foam block
Cinnamon sticks
Silver birch twigs
Stub wires
Wax gilt
Hot glue
Fresh ivy

I remain firmly in favour of natural materials, but this does not always mean that I use evergreens for my designs. The Christmas wreath illustrated in this chapter uses an olive wood garland as its base and this has been decorated with groups of pine cones, golden mushrooms and small terracotta pots filled with cinnamon sticks and silver birch twigs. Lengths of fresh ivy with gilded leaves have been twined around the garland to contrast with the earthy tones of the rest of the design. Except for the ivy, this wreath can be prepared well in advance which is a bonus for those of us with busy lives.

Strictly speaking, this is not a dried flower project, but as I would not recommend using dried flowers outside, I hope some flexibility is acceptable.

Should you wish to make a wreath incorporating greenery, you will find that the simple moss ring is a useful base and that bunches of pine, holly and ivy can be pinned to it using floral pins or stub wires. Once Christmas is over, the evergreens can be removed and the moss ring can be stored for next Christmas or used to make another dried flower garland, adding new greenery as wished.

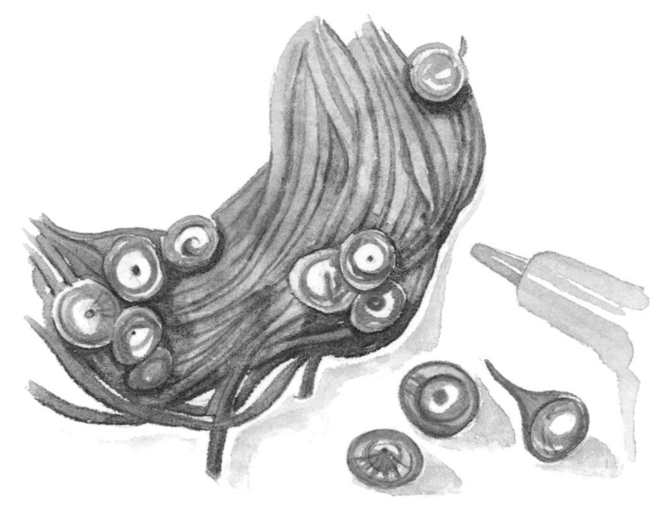

1 Using a length of stub wire, make a strong loop to hang the wreath. Pass another length of stub wire through the hole in the bottom of the flowerpots and secure them to the olive wood wreath. Arrange groups of pine cones in the spaces between the flowerpots. When you are happy with the arrangement, glue the pine cones in place.

2 Gild the golden mushrooms and silver birch twigs by applying the wax gilt with your finger or with a soft cloth. Fix groups of golden mushrooms to the wreath using the glue gun.

3 Cut a small piece of dry foam to fit each flowerpot and then cover the foam with a layer of sheet moss.

A skilfully woven olive wood ring is the base for this Christmas garland. Decorated with pine cones, gilded mushrooms and tiny pots filled with twigs and bark it is twined with fresh ivy to make a country-style door decoration. When it is time to refresh the garland change the mood with cinnamon sticks, twists of dried orange peel, apple rings and dried cranberries.

4 Fill two of the flowerpots with bark and the other two with twigs. Do this by pushing the bark or twigs through the moss into the foam.

5 When you are ready to hang the wreath, twine lengths of fresh ivy around the garland and gild the occasional leaf with the wax gilt.

Woodland garland

The varied textures and soft silvers, greys and greens of mosses and lichens make them irresistible materials for this woodland garland. The wreath begins as a simple moss ring; with the addition of twigs, cones and barks, the garland becomes a collage of all that is wonderful about a walk in the woods. My urban friends love to hang this memento of rural life on their walls as a reminder of the natural world beyond the city limits.

Most of the materials that I have used for this project are bought from suppliers who obtain them from renewable sources. I do not recommend the plundering of woodlands for supplies as many of these materials are important in the natural ecological chain. However, there is no reason why you should not pick up the occasional fallen cone, twig or piece of bark to add character to your arrangement.

I have used five varieties of mosses and lichens on this garland, carpet moss, bun moss, natural lichen, Spanish moss (*Tilancia*) and oakmoss which in spite of its name is in fact a lichen. Some of these may be readily available at your florist or local nursery. Oakmoss may be more of a problem, it is chiefly used in perfumes and pot-pourri and is obtainable from botanical suppliers and herbalists.

Do not try for symmetry in this design, it should not look arranged but rather as if it just grew. Gather your materials around you and experiment with interesting groupings and once you are happy with the colours and textures build your design on the moss ring. It may look a bit bland at first, but once you start to add the twigs and cones, all the materials will contrast wonderfully with one another and the garland will take on a life of its own.

MATERIALS

Prepared moss ring (see page 80)
1 bag each of:
Bun moss
Lichen
Spanish moss
Oakmoss

Cones
Bark
Twigs
Floral pins or stub wires
Hot glue

1 Pin and glue a piece of bun moss on to the moss garland and then build up around it with the other mosses, glueing or pinning them as necessary.

2 Repeat this process with the other mosses and lichens, working your way around the ring, until the whole surface is covered.

3 Add the cones, twigs and bark as your finishing touches, securing the more unwieldy pieces with wire or pins as well as dabs of hot glue.

Bun moss, flat moss, Spanish moss and natural lichen are available from dried flower shops, but you may need to visit a herbalist for oakmoss, and don't forget to look for mosses in your garden.

Herb garland

Each summer, I harvest herbs from my garden and hang them up to dry in my kitchen. They look, and smell, wonderful but ideally they should only stay there as long as it takes to dry them thoroughly; at which time they should be stripped from their stems and stored in glass jars away from strong light. However, I do miss the fragrant bundles when they are gone so I have designed this simple and attractive herb garland to take their place.

The subtle pinks, greys and silvers of the herbs on this twiggy garland are complemented by the colour-washed background, but it would look equally at home in more sophisticated surroundings. When giving this garland as a gift, include separate cotton bags of the culinary herbs so the recipient doesn't need to raid the garland for bay leaves and thyme.

Using a vine or fernleaf wreath as the base, I wire and glue bundles of fragrant herbs to the ring until all that is visible is an aromatic mass of oregano, marjoram, sage, artemesia and bay. Any herb that dries well is suitable for this garland and once you have made one, you may well find that, like myself, you will be commissioned to make more for your friends.

MATERIALS

Vine or fernleaf wreath
Generous bundles of herbs eg thyme, marjoram, sage, savory
Fine reel wire
Stub wire
Hot glue
Brass or plastic ring

1 *Wrap the reel wire around the wreath a couple of times and then thread the brass or plastic ring on to the wire and fasten it off securely.*

2 *Using the reel wire, bind together a few stems of each herb to make little bunches. You will need about eight bunches of four varieties. The bunches should be roughly 10 cm (4 in) in length.*

3 *Using the stub wire, attach each bundle firmly to the base of the garland, working your way round the circle with the herbs pointing in the same direction. If you have difficulty wiring the herbs firmly in place, use a glue gun for added security.*

Baskets

Baskets of all shapes and sizes have always attracted me, and I am known to buy them for no other reason than they simply look so appealing. Of course, baskets and dried flowers go hand-in-hand, and in this chapter I have used a variety of basket designs, including an unusual display with a Chinese steamer basket. Boxes, too, are ideal containers and are perhaps overlooked for dried flowers. Pretty shapes such as oval or heart-shaped boxes make lovely gifts when scented and filled with a selection of plump flowerheads and pretty foliage.

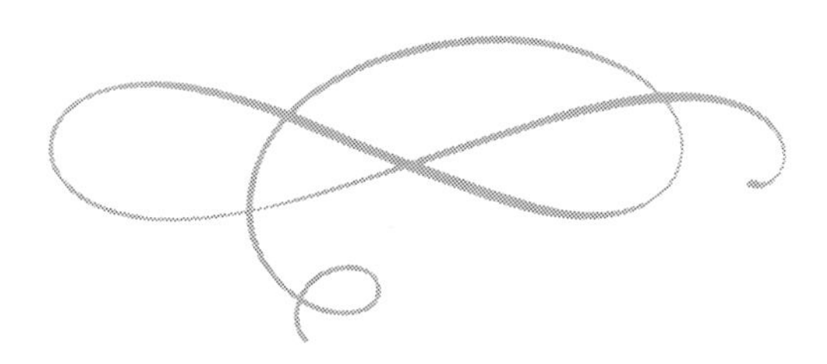

Vivid hues combine in this midsummer basket. Choose contrasting colours when you're looking for a dramatic effect.

I love baskets and boxes and use them throughout my house for practical and decorative purposes as well as for my dried flower arrangements. Most of the materials that I work with must be stored away or they will deteriorate, but baskets are the exception and I consider them worthy of display in their own right and hang numbers of them from my kitchen ceiling as well as pressing them into temporary service as useful receptacles for fruit, houseplants and even the occasional sleeping cat!

I am an impulse shopper when it comes to baskets, and will frequently buy one for its inherent beauty rather than because it is ideal for a project I have in mind, and some become such favourites that I find excuses not to use them, even though they are suitable.

These days the people of the Philippines are the acknowledged masters of basket-making, producing highly original and well-made baskets woven from local materials such as vines, twigs, roots, leaves and mosses. Most of this work is done in rural villages and is a vital source of income as well as ensuring that these traditional skills are kept alive.

With their natural colours and textures, baskets make particularly sympathetic containers for dried flower arrangements of any size; from a tiny basket of flowers decorating a birthday cake to a huge basket brim full of vibrant flowers, brightening a winter room.

I find that rustic unvarnished baskets fit well into most surroundings, but if you find them too plain for your taste, they can be painted, stained or varnished in a satin finish.

Decorative boxes come in all shapes and sizes these days. In particular, papier mâché is enjoying a revival, and is sometimes sold unpainted in a natural light brown which complements the dried flowers in the same way as baskets and old terracotta. If you can't get hold of papier mâché, make your own version by covering a suitable sized cardboard box or tin with thick brown wrapping paper with the matt side facing outwards, or if you want something more colourful use a piece of wallpaper. It is also worth keeping a look out for interesting boxes with missing lids that are on sale cheaply in stores or junk shops. Why pay for a lid that you won't use?

A basket of dried flowers is an acceptable gift for most occasions. Just take a look at the displays in the shops for Mother's Day, Easter, Christmas and the many other times during the year when the retailers are in hot pursuit of our money. Making your own basket arrangement is much more personal and can turn an acceptable gift into a coveted and prized one.

Top: The vibrant colours of the flowers in these steamer baskets are a wonderful surprise when the lid is lifted. For an even more dramatic effect paint the basket black before adding the flowers. Below left: pastel colours nestle in this country basket of more subtle hues.

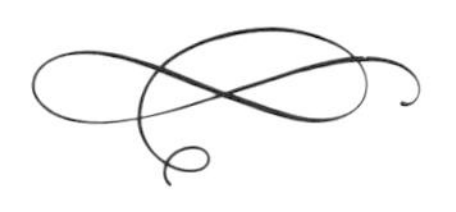

Wheat basket

Wheat is an easy material to work with and inexpensive to buy, so when I use it in a basket I like to really cram it in for a 'bounteous harvest' effect. I have used an old-fashioned bicycle basket for this project. Its high sides are in good proportion to the long stems and its colour and texture harmonise well with the soft green wheat. Don't insert more than 6 or 8 stalks at once or some of the stalks will bend and spoil the symmetry of the arrangement.

MATERIALS

Bicycle basket
4 bunches wheat
3 dry foam blocks
Bundle natural raffia

The clean symmetrical lines of the wheat are complemented by the simple willow basket. A twist of raffia finished with a large bow adds a suitably rustic flourish to the arrangement. For a more sophisticated effect use a Regency-style urn instead of a basket.

1 Using a long-bladed knife, cut the foam to shape and fit it into the basket so that it sits 3 cm (1 in) below the front lip of the basket.

2 To attach the raffia, thread six pieces approximately 25 cm (10 in) long through the walls of the basket just below its lip. Take half the bundle of raffia and, starting at the back of the basket, tie it in place twisting it round on itself to form a rope as you work.

3 Trim the raffia ties to 1 cm (1/2 in) long. Then tie the two ends of the raffia rope together at the front, trimming the ends to 10 cm (4 in) long.

4 Now take the rest of the bundle of raffia and tie it in the middle with a single piece of raffia. Form a loop of raffia either side of the knot and tie it in the centre to form a bow. Trim the ends of the raffia and tie the bow on to the front of the basket.

Raffia is a wonderful natural material with which to work. If you prefer something a little different, use dyed raffia which is available in a variety of colours.

5 Starting at the back, begin to fill the basket with wheat. At this point the height of the wheat above the basket should be approximately the same as the height of the basket itself. Arrange a line of wheat along the back of the basket taking time to ensure that it is level.

6 Work forwards, keeping the wheat at the same level until the basket is half full and then gradually begin to shorten the stems as you work forwards until you reach the front of the basket, where the bottom of the wheat ears should be approximately 10 cm (4 in) above the rim.

Midsummer basket

I smiled while I was making this arrangement. Outside it was a gloomy winter's day, but inside it was a riot of colour as I worked with a wonderful selection of flowers; yellow achillea, sunflowers and chrysanthemum, gold and orange dahlias, blue larkspur and green safflowers. By using the strongly contrasting yellows and blues the colours are intensified and the flowers look as if they have been freshly picked.

MATERIALS

20 cm (8 in) rustic basket
1½ dry foam blocks
1 bunch sunflowers
2 bunches safflowers
1 bunch deep blue larkspur
2 bunches *Achillea filipendulina*
1 bunch chrysanthemum
8–10 dahlias
Stub wires

This impressionistic arrangement is full of colour and vitality, by placing the blues and yellows next to one another they become much brighter than when used separately.

Underneath all the flowers is a small rustic basket just 20 cm (8 in) wide, but by the time the flowers have been added, the finished arrangement has doubled in width. When you are buying baskets it is worth bearing in mind that the basket should be roughly half the size of the finished arrangement.

To give the flowers height I have built up the dry foam in the basket, so that it stands above the rim. The flowers all have relatively short stems which means that I have much more control over their placement.

When making medium-size or large, mixed arrangements you will find that the best results are obtained by grouping numbers of the same flowers together. This creates blocks of colour; by placing flowers individually, the arrangement can look 'bitty' and lose its impact.

1 Using a long-bladed knife, cut the block of foam to fit the basket. Cut the half block of foam in half again lengthwise and place one of the pieces on the foam in the basket and pin it into place using stub wires.

2 Place your first flowers centrally in the basket. They should be approximately the same height above the basket as the height of the basket itself.

3 Work towards the edge of the basket grouping flowers together. When you reach the outside edges of the basket start to angle the stems of the flowers as you place them in the foam so that you create the arrangement's curving outline. Be careful to ensure that the flowers cover the edge of the basket or the foam may be visible if the arrangement is viewed from the side.

Achieve a densely packed display by keeping the stems relatively short and grouping the different varieties together. This basket uses a considerable amount of material, don't forget that a larger basket would need even more.

Pastel basket

The soft green of this basket is a perfect foil for the delicate colours of this arrangement. The use of pink and yellow together is fairly unusual but works well with the soft tones of the peonies and *Achillea verticor*. The green safflowers combine well with the other flowers, while its pointed, slightly prickly shape provides an interesting contrast to the flat achillea heads.

MATERIALS

20 cm (8 in) oval basket
2 bunches yellow *Achillea verticor*
1 bunch pink *Achillea verticor*
1 bunch pink spray roses
1 bunch safflowers
6 peony heads
Dry foam block

I have arranged the flowers so that they tumble over the edge of the basket; this breaks up the straight lines of the basket and ensures that all the stems and the foam are concealed when the display is viewed from the side. As you work, it is worth checking all round, it may look terrific from above but reveal unsightly stalks and foam when viewed from the side.

I bought this basket ready painted, but if the right colour is not available I paint my own using thinned down emulsion paint. It gives a light matt covering which looks great with most flowers and allows the texture and grain of the wood to show through.

The low shape of this basket and the spreading outline of the flowers make this an ideal table centrepiece. Dried flowers are perfect for this purpose, they can be arranged ahead of time, there is no worrying about water marks on the table and they can be used over and over again.

If a dining room is not used daily, I recommend that the flowers are packed away. There are two reasons for this; first the flowers will retain their colour longer and get less dusty, and secondly they will be more pleasing to you if they are not on view all the time. Alternatively, for a room that is in regular use, have two arrangements, one for everyday and one for special occasions.

A sympathetic container is an essential part of a good arrangement. Here the oval wooden basket is painted a soft green which blends well with the delicate colours of the flowers, and its outline is echoed by the shape of the arrangement which tumbles gently over its sides.

1 Using a long-bladed knife, cut the foam to fit the basket. The top of the foam should be level with the rim of the basket.

2 Place a group of achillea *heads slightly off centre and then build your arrangement outwards from this point. The central flowers should be approximately the same height above the basket as the height of the basket itself. With the exception of the peonies you should work with groups of the same flowers rather than individual flowerheads.*

3 As you work towards the outer edges of the basket angle the stems so that you create a curving outline, and place some of the flowers so that they hang over the rim of the basket.

Wall basket

Where space is limited, a wall basket is an ideal solution. This colourful arrangement combines strong pinks and reds of peonies and roses with deep blue larkspur and green *Nigella orientalis*. The pink flowers are emphasised by the addition of the cerise pink bow which adds interest to the basket if it is viewed at eye level. The *Nigella* bursts exuberantly from the basket, and together with the pale green leaves, gives the arrangement strong outward and upward movement. A softer effect would result if you used safflowers.

MATERIALS

Flat backed basket approximately 20 cm (8 in) wide
2 dry foam blocks
2 bunches safflowers
1 bunch salal or holly oak leaves
1 bunch deep blue larkspur
1 bunch pink roses
1 bunch red roses
8 peonies
60 cm (24 in) of 5 cm (2 in) wide ribbon
Hot glue

A flat backed basket is equally useful for wall or table top displays and has the great advantage that it uses half the number of flowers of a conventional arrangement. This basket has deep pink peonies and roses and blue larkspur nestling amongst spiky green Nigella orientalis, *with pale green leaves softening the outline.*

1 *Using a long-bladed knife, cut a block of foam to fit the basket. The foam should stand 5 cm (2 in) above the rim of the basket.*

2 *Arrange a row of flowers along the back of the basket. Fan the flowers out as you work towards the outside edges to establish the curved shape of the arrangement. Viewed from behind, the flowers should stand 10 cm (4 in) above the back edge of the basket.*

3 *Work forwards, adding groups of flowers, and individual peonies. As you reach the front of the basket, angle the stalks to conceal the rim of the basket.*

4 *Make a simple bow with the ribbon (see page 123) and glue it in place. Glue a few rosebuds to the centre of the bow.*

Hydrangea basket

This rather wild and wonderful moss and wire basket was perfect for the hydrangea arrangement, although something more restrained would also work well. It is simplicity itself and for anyone with hydrangeas in the garden it will also be very economical.

MATERIALS

Basket approximately 40 cm (15 in) wide × 20 cm (8 in) high

25–30 hydrangea heads

3–4 dry foam blocks

Newspaper

Stub wires

It can be time consuming and very expensive to create large scale dried flower arrangements, but hydrangeas are the exception. The flowerheads are large, readily available and look wonderful when massed together as they are in this moss and chicken wire basket. A moss lined wirework hanging basket will also look wonderful.

The full and generous flowerheads of hydrangeas are particularly successful in large baskets, and relatively few flowers go a long way.

When working with large baskets, I fill the bulk of the basket with crumpled newspaper before finishing with a layer of florists' foam which is firmly wedged into the basket to prevent it moving about. In this case I have also built up the foam in the centre of the basket to give the arrangement height.

1 Fill the bottom half of the basket with tightly crumpled newspaper. Place dry florists' foam on top of the newspaper. Wedge it into the sides of the basket to stop it moving about. If necessary fill in around the sides with smaller pieces of foam.

2 Build up with further foam in the centre of the basket using bent stub wires to hold the foam in place. It should stand roughly 15 cm (6 in) above the rim of the basket.

3 Arrange the hydrangeas in the foam, starting in the middle of the basket and packing the flowerheads closely together. If the stems are too short, twist stub wire around the stem to give them extended length.

4 Curve the line of the flowers downwards as you work towards the edge of the basket and make sure that at the rim there is a generous overhang of hydrangea heads.

Burgundy and green basket

Last summer I was very excited to discover these wonderful burgundy lupins and felt inspired to design an arrangement around them. I decided to keep the arrangement quite simple and with a strong colour theme. I selected deep red peonies and purple-red oregano to tone well with the lupins. These glorious burgundy colours I offset with the green tones of safflowers, pale green leaves and poppy seedheads.

MATERIALS

30 cm (12 in) oval basket
2 bunches lupins
10 deep red peonies
1 bunch oregano
2 bunches poppy seedheads
1 bunch salal or holly oak leaves
2 bunches green safflowers
2 dry foam blocks
stub wires

This is a fairly large arrangement using a 30 cm (12 in) bird's nest basket and, with the flowers, the finished design is 50 cm (20 in) wide.

Making an arrangement this size can be an expensive business, but in this case I have kept the costs down by using green as the majority colour, although the stronger burgundy tones are visually dominant. Green leaves, buds and seedheads are inexpensive to buy and make excellent fillers in dried flower arrangements.

I have built up the florist's foam in the basket to give the flowers height and then working from the middle I have completed first one side of the basket and then the other. I find it easier to achieve a balanced result working this way.

Before I start, I divide the materials into two piles to ensure that there is an even distribution of flowers throughout the arrangement.

A basket this size is an impressive gift. I have given a number to friends as wedding presents and over the years the baskets are returned to me for re-vamping as the flowers fade or colour schemes change.

If you are unable to obtain lupins, you could substitute *Amaranthus*.

Limiting the colours used in an arrangement helps to create a balanced design. The burgundy flowers and green seedheads and foliage used in this bird's nest basket are a sophisticated combination which is given added interest by the varied textures.

1 Place one block of foam in the bottom of the basket. Cut the other block in half lengthwise and pin one half to the foam in the basket. Use the remainder of the foam to fill in around the edges.

2 Insert two peonies just off centre and build the other flowers and foliage around them working on one half of the basket at a time.

3 Group flowers and foliage of the same variety together for greater impact, with the exception of the lupins and the salal or holly oak leaves which stand slightly above the line of the arrangement to create an interesting outline.

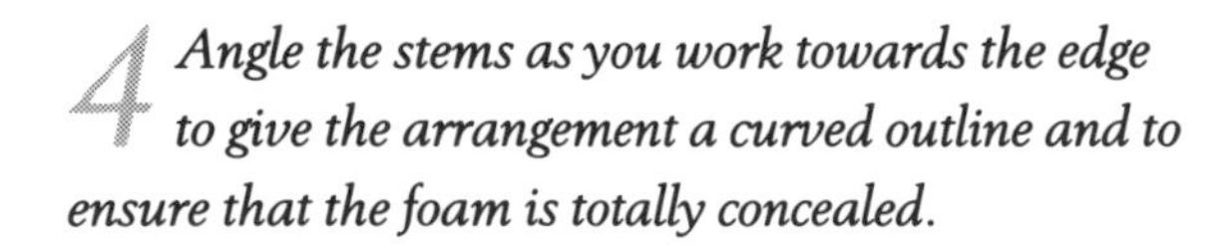

4 Angle the stems as you work towards the edge to give the arrangement a curved outline and to ensure that the foam is totally concealed.

Deep burgundy peonies, lupins and marjoram combine with green safflowers, poppy heads and salal or hollyoak leaves to create a richly textured tapestry.

Box of delights

A couple of years ago a cosmetic company asked me to help them design a Christmas gift line which used a Chinese steamer basket containing their products. While working on this project I realised that I could use these baskets for scented dried flower arrangements.

MATERIALS

Chinese steamer basket with two layers
Selection of flowers in two colour themes
Dry foam block
Perfume oil of your choice
Hot glue

I love to use jewel-coloured flowers in my arrangements, but I accept that they will inevitably fade when they are exposed to the light. The steamer basket offered an opportunity to arrange flowers in an attractive container with a woven top which allows fragrance to permeate even when the lid is in place. Concealed in the layers of the basket are two dazzling dried flower collages which can be revealed when the room is in use and protected at other times by the lid.

This basket makes a wonderful gift with its hidden surprises. As it is unwrapped and friends exclaim 'A Chinese Steamer Basket!' you can sit back and wait for the inevitable moment when they lift the lid.

Dazzling pink blooms are crammed into one layer of a Chinese steamer basket.

The techniques involved in making this arrangement are very simple. It is the colour and variety of the flowers that gives it its excitement. This is an ideal opportunity to use a few precious blooms to maximum effect.

For instance, I have used some wonderful freeze-dried roses which I rarely use because of their expense, fragility and because they fade very quickly when exposed to the light. For the pink collage I have also included vibrant cerise celosia, purple dahlias, marjoram, peonies and tiny roses. The yellow collage consists of pale yellow freeze-dried roses, ordinary deep yellow roses, achillea, sunflowers and chrysanthemum. The basket is scented with Summer Garden perfume oil.

I really enjoy the intense hues of the collages, but softer shades work equally well.

These gloriously vivid flowers are more of a collage than a dried flower arrangement, with the design built from one side of the basket to the other.

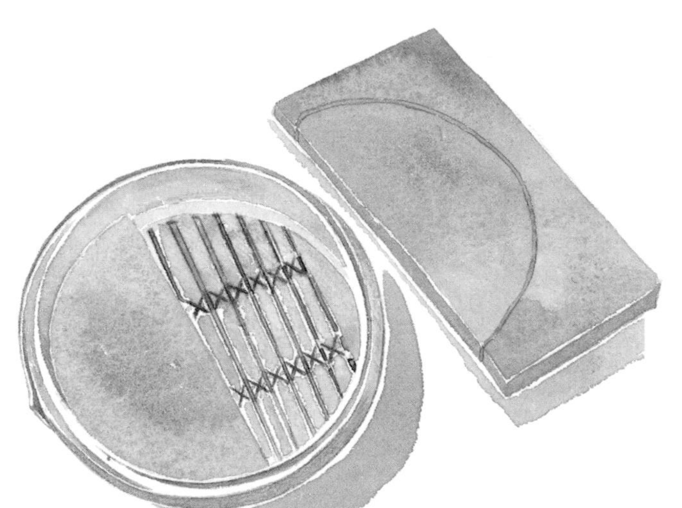

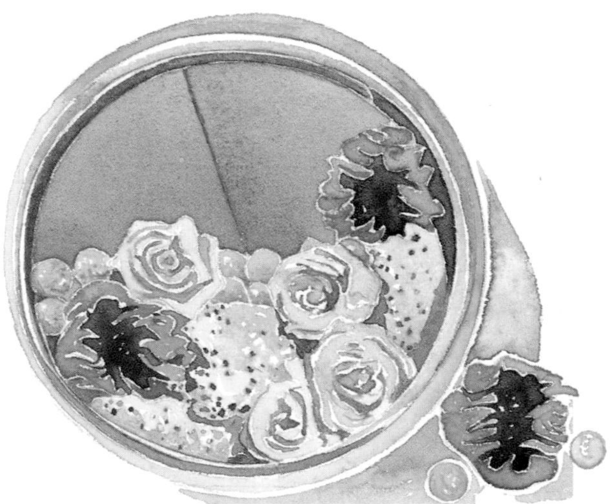

1 Using a long-bladed knife, cut the foam into four slices, lengthwise. Place two slices of foam alongside one another and, using the lid of the box as a template, cut the foam to fit the box. Repeat this process with the other two pieces of foam.

2 Using a glue gun, stick the foam to the bottom of each layer of the basket. Scent each layer with 5 drops of perfume oil.

3 Place your first flower against the side of the basket and work across to the other side, glueing the flowers in place once you are happy with their position. Place small flowers together in groups rather than positioning them individually.

Scented Valentine's box

I love surprises and this design is based on the assumption that there are lots of people who feel the same. What appears to be a simple decorated box, reveals its secret when the lid is lifted. Inside is a bed of vibrant green scented moss outlined with roses. Use it to fragrance a room. When the flowers are past their best, you can use the box for other purposes.

On a visit to one of my suppliers, I spied these heart-shaped papier mâché boxes and bought a set to experiment with. When I got home I realised that one had a nasty mark on the lid, and rather than paint the box, I draped tartan ribbon across it at various angles.

At this point I could have left them as simple storage boxes but I had just received some particularly lush looking moss which looked wonderful in the box. The roses were added and the arrangement was scented with tea rose oil to make this a perfect Valentine's Day gift.

MATERIALS

Heart-shaped box approximately 20 cm (8 in) wide

1.5 m (60 in) of 25 mm (1 in) wide tartan ribbon

Moss

20 red roses

Tea rose oil

Dry foam block

Hot glue

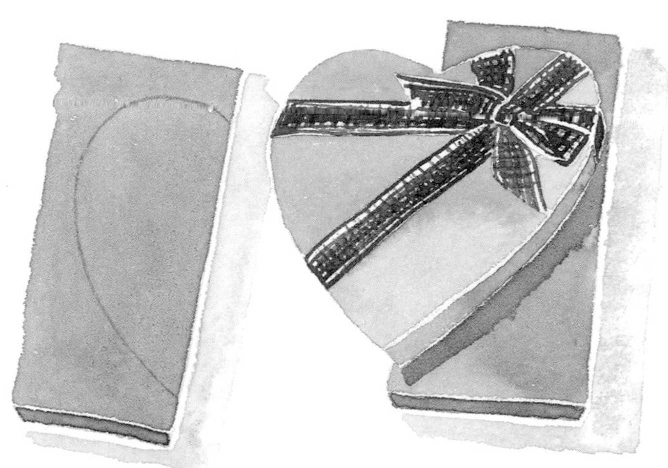

This message of love can be used long after Valentine's Day as a cache for favourite earrings and brooches.

1 Position ribbon across the top of the lid, down either side and inside the lid; cut it to the correct length and glue it in place. Now position a second piece of ribbon diagonally across the lid. Cut the ribbon to length and glue it in place also.

2 Tie a simple bow with the remainder of the ribbon, cutting the tails at an angle. Glue the bow in place where the two ribbons meet.

3 Using the long-bladed knife, cut two 3 cm (1 in) slices, lengthwise, off the block of foam. Press one half of the lid of the box into the piece of foam so that the outline of the heart shows clearly. Repeat this procedure with the other slice of foam.

4 Now cut the foam following the impressed outline and use the two pieces to line the box. Scent the foam with 5 drops of perfume oil.

5 Take the lid of the box and lay it on to the moss. Cut round the moss to fit the box. (You may need to patch pieces together if your piece is not quite big enough.)

6 Trim the roses, leaving only a short length of stem on each one. Apply glue to the base of each flowerhead and push them into position around the edge of the box.

Practicalities

FLOWERS FOR DRYING

Few of us have gardens of sufficient size to grow all the flowers needed by the dried flower arranger, so I would recommend that you restrict yourself to growing easily cultivated specimens like hydrangea and achillea, old-fashioned varieties such as peonies, old garden roses and hellebores which when dried are very expensive to buy, and as many of the aromatic herbs as you have room for, including lavender, marjoram, bergamot, sage and thyme. Remember though that, with the exception of the hydrangea, you will be picking these flowers at their best, so if you want to avoid the garden looking bare, you might like to plant extra blooms.

Obviously conditions vary and you will need to take into account your location and soil type and adjust accordingly.

DRYING YOUR OWN FLOWERS

When you begin drying your own flowers you won't need any special equipment. Start small, with just one bunch of flowers or even a single bloom. Don't be put off if you haven't seen a particular flower dried before, the great advantage of drying flowers at home is that you can try out flowers that the commercial growers find uneconomical or haven't yet considered. For instance, a recent discovery of mine has been the delightful moss-rose. These dry beautifully and the moss stays a vivid, emerald green. It is unlikely that these lovely flowers will ever be available in the shops so there is the added enjoyment of their exclusivity.

Air Drying

Establish the best place in your house for drying; some flowers dry best in warm dry conditions such as an airing cupboard or over a kitchen range or central heating boiler, others prefer a cool, well-ventilated room. Some will dry perfectly well in either spot but look quite different when dry. Warm air drying generally results in a crisper appearance and more intense colour while cool air drying gives a softer look and more muted colours. Whichever method you use the flowers should be hung away from strong light to avoid fading. It is essential that you experiment for yourself as conditions can vary enormously from one house to another.

The weather is also an important factor, a wet spell can turn your usually cool dry shed into a humid, mould-inducing, disaster area. Obviously, it is not a good idea to start drying flowers in poor weather, but if you are caught mid-way through the process it is a good idea to have a back-up warm spot to where you can move the flowers. An oven on a very low heat can also be used to save the day.

Whether the flowers are from your own garden or bought, they should be in the best possible condition. Flowers should be picked on a dry day when the dew has evaporated. They should be in full bloom, but only just or they will start to drop their petals as they dry.

The actual drying process is extremely simple. Remove most of the leaves, and hang the flowers upside down – in small bunches for slender blooms such as lavender or love-in-the-mist and individually for larger fleshier flowers like peonies and delphiniums. Herbs benefit from being wrapped in cones of newspaper, prior to hanging up as this prevents the leaves curling as they dry. A purpose-made rack or an old fashioned ceiling-hung airer are ideal and can be very decorative, but I have managed very well in the past with Heath Robinson constructions made from garden canes and string.

The length of time it takes a flower to dry depends on the moisture in the flower and in the air but generally when the stem is dry and rigid the flower is ready to be stored or used.

Air drying

Herb cones

Drying peonies

I am often asked about drying peonies, and it is certainly true that they are a little trickier than other flowers, because of their size and the density of the petals. They should be fully open when they are hung up to dry, but not overblown or they will drop their petals.

Hang them individually, or in bunches of three at the most, with their heads at different levels to one another. They need warm air to dry successfully. Once they are dry to the touch (5–7 days) take them down and stand them upright in vases close to the source of heat for a couple of weeks to allow any residual moisture to evaporate. Experience has taught me that there is often a very wet spell of weather around the time that I dry my peonies, so if necessary I will leave them in the warm air for a longer period. They can then be stored between layers of tissue paper in boxes. It is a good idea to include some sachets of dessicant to absorb atmospheric moisture as well as a sachet of moth repellent to prevent any possible insect damage.

Most flowers respond very well to this method of air drying but there are a couple of exceptions. Gypsophila and hydrangeas dry better stood with water and left until the water has evaporated. Hydrangeas should not be picked from the garden until they start to change colour in the autumn and the flowers become leathery.

Drying with dessicants

As you gain experience, you will find that certain flowers dry less successfully than others and you may wish to try other drying methods. There are various mediums that can be used, sand is the cheapest and most easily available and silica gel or clay granules, the modern equivalent. Flower stems do not dry successfully by this method so you will need to insert a wire inside the stalk or wire it externally if you wish to use the flowers in an arrangement.

Dessicants work by drawing the moisture from the flowers into the surrounding drying medium. It is essential to make sure that the sand, gel or granules are totally dry before use and this is best achieved by leaving them in a warm oven for 4 hours or for 10 minutes at medium heat in a microwave. Only one variety of flower should be dried at a time as drying times vary; for example, multi-petalled varieties take longer.

Place a rack or a piece of wire netting in the bottom of the container and gently rest the flowers on this. Drizzle the sand, gel or granules around each bloom being careful to support the petals in as lifelike a position as possible. The flowers must be fully covered. Place in a warm dry place and the flowers should be dry in 3–5 days. They are far more fragile than air dried flowers, fade faster and have a tendency to re-absorb moisture but, in spite of this, it is a technique that is worth the effort because the flowers will retain many of the qualities they had when fresh and can be used to stunning effect for a special occasion. Spraying them with one of the proprietary dried flower protector sprays will help prolong their life.

Microwave drying

Quick, easy and very successful for small quantities. As microwaves vary in strength it is necessary to experiment for yourself on drying times, but as a guide line, I dry 3 bunches of lavender or other herbs at medium strength for 3–4 minutes.

Do keep an eye on aromatic herbs when you dry them this way as it is possible for the volatile oils to vaporise and catch fire. This has only happened to me once, and I have found no one else who has experienced anything similar, but if you are of a nervous disposition you may prefer to confine the use of the microwave to less aromatic flowers!

A microwave oven can also be used to dry flowers in silica gel or dessicant, and again you will need to establish drying times suitable for your own particular microwave. As a general guideline, flowers seem to dry best on defrost or the lowest temperature setting.

Pack the blooms in the dessicant as described above, placing the flowers on crumpled paper towel rather than a metal rack. For the container, I use a cardboard box without its lid. Set the timer for 3–4 minutes and leave the flowers to stand for 15 minutes afterwards and then check to see if they are dry. Adjust the timing as you feel necessary.

STORING DRIED FLOWERS

Once your flowers are fully dry they should be removed from the source of heat or they will over dry and become very brittle.

The best way to store them is packed between layers of tissue paper in cardboard boxes. Your local florist throws away lots of suitable boxes daily and will probably be happy to let you have some for nothing.

I always add a few sachets of dessicant and some moth repellent as well to prevent the possibility of insect damage while the flowers are in storage. The boxes are then stowed away in a cool, dry place. A garden shed or garage is not recommended as these tend to get quite damp in autumn and winter.

PROLONGING THE LIFE OF YOUR DRIED FLOWERS

Contrary to the opinions of some, the use of dried flowers in the home need not mean that you are espousing the Miss Havisham style of interior decoration where faded relics festooned with cobwebs gather dust at an alarming rate.

Sprays are now available which will help preserve the colour of the flowers and repel the dust. I use these on completed arrangements and then occasionally blow a cool hairdryer over the display to remove any dust.

The natural life of a dried flower arrangement should be 1–2 years, after which it should be thrown away. One of the reasons that dried flowers developed such a bad reputation in the past was because people held on to aged arrangements for far too long. Of course, you may love the faded flowers. I have a friend who asks me to pass my 'mature' arrangements on to her rather than throw them away!

STEAMING DRIED FLOWERS

During storage, flowers can become misshapen but this can be remedied by holding the flower over steam from a boiling kettle. I also use this method to open up roses, which tend to close as they dry. I hold the bloom over the steam until it visibly softens and then use a piece of wire to gently re-position the petals.

EQUIPMENT

Certain materials and equipment are essential for the dried flower arranger. Most are easily available. If you have difficulty obtaining a particular item, ask for help from your local flower arranging club or check the classified section of craft magazines for mail order suppliers. I have not listed every item used in this book, but this list covers the basic equipment you will need to get started. I would recommend that you read each project carefully before you start work to check that you have all the materials needed.

GLUE GUNS

I consider this an essential. These are available from do-it-yourself outlets, department stores and craft suppliers. It is worth buying one with a trigger action if you are planning to do a lot of work, and look out for the new low temperature glue guns which avoid the risk of nasty burns if you are careless with the hot glue.

Hot glue dries very quickly and anchors items really securely.

GLUE STICKS

These white, pliable sticks are the ammunition for the glue gun. They slot into the gun and one end melts with the heat on to your item to be glued. You should buy the sticks that are used for cellulose ie wood and paper.

STUB WIRE

Rigid pieces of wire of varying lengths and thicknesses. In green, brown or silver. Used where sturdy fixings are required.

FINE REEL WIRE

Used for all fine work. Available in silver or green. Cut with scissors.

FLORAL PINS

U-shaped wire pins with sharpened points, very useful for garlands. If they are not available in your area, stub wires can be bent and cut to shape as a substitute.

DRY FLORISTS' FOAM

Available in blocks, spheres and cones, it forms the base for most dried flower arrangements.

MOULDING POWDER OR PLASTER OF PARIS

Used for setting the base and giving stability to tall arrangements such as topiary trees. Available from art or craft shops.

SCISSORS

Strong all-purpose scissors are suitable for most projects. Ones with a notch for cutting wire are also useful.

KNIFE

For cutting florists' foam to shape, a long-bladed knife is useful.

How to use a glue gun
Insert a glue stick into the gun, plug it in and leave it for a few minutes to heat up. When you are ready to use the gun simply press the trigger and glue will emerge from the nozzle. When glueing flowers, be sure to glue the stem or the base of the flower rather than the petals, otherwise the flower will soon work loose. As you work, you will find that the melted glue tends to form fine strands that get caught in the flowers and foliage. Lift these off as you go or the finished arrangement may look as if it has been visited by an overactive spider.

Wiring flowerheads
Where flowers have shorter stems than required or where a stem has snapped off, stub wires can be used to create a stem. Push a wire through the head of the flower near its base. Push a second wire through at right angles to the first. Fold the wires back under the head of the flower and twist them round on themselves.

Wiring a flowerpot
Insert a stub wire through the base of the pot, and twist the ends of the wire together at the rim of the pot. Take a second wire and repeat the process, but this time twist the ends together at the base of the pot. Use the two wires to attach the pot to the garland.

Wiring a flower

Wiring a flowerpot

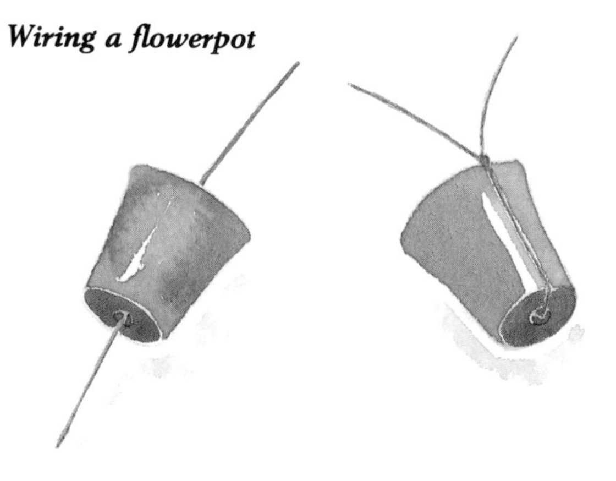

Making bows
Making bows is not difficult if you have the technique. The following two bows will give professional results, and have the added advantage that you do not need to cut the ribbon from the roll before you start, so there is no wastage.

SIMPLE BOW
For a perfect bow every time you will need a flower pot, dry foam, two sticks and, of course, the ribbon.

Fit the foam in to the pot and push the sticks into the foam. Wrap the ribbon around the two sticks, then pass one end under the other as if you are knotting a tie. Loop it over the ribbon at the back and bring it forwards. Now loop it around the length of ribbon that is hanging in front and pull tight. Trim the tails to the required length.

This method will work for any width of ribbon, but you will need to place the sticks further apart for bigger bows.

DOUBLE BOW
Make a figure-of-eight by holding the tail of the ribbon in one hand and with the other hand bring the ribbon over towards you and then under and away. Repeat this movement so that the bow now has 4 loops. Pinch the bow in the middle and fasten with fine reel wire. Cut the tails at an angle to finish.

Simple bow

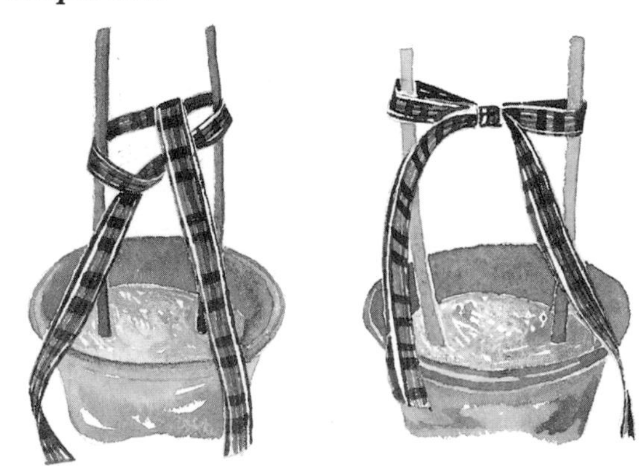

Double bow

Colour options

With a few exceptions, I have tried to use easily available dried flowers for the projects in this book, and where I have used more unusual materials I have suggested alternatives in the chart below.

From the vast range of dried flowers on sale I have selected those I use most frequently. As you become more experienced and enthusiastic you may well wish to add to this list.

WHITE/SILVER/GREY

Gypsophila (white)
Achillea, The Pearl (white)
Achillea verticor white (white)
Artemesia (silver)
Natural lichen (silver)
Oak moss (grey)
Spanish moss (*Tilancia*) (grey)
Poppy seedheads (grey)
Sage (grey)

BLUE

Larkspur (light and dark blue)
Lavender French (dark blue)
Lavender English (grey blue)

GREEN

Safflower (*Carthamus sp.*)
Nigella orientalis
Wheat
Marjoram
Hydrangea (white heads dry to green)
Salal leaves (substitute holly oak leaves)
Sheet moss
Bun moss

YELLOW

Rose 'Golden Time' (deep yellow)
Achillea filipendulina (deep yellow)
Sunflower (*Helianthus*) (deep yellow)
Chrysanthemum (bright yellow)
Craspedia (bright yellow)
Dahlia (pale yellow)
Helichrysum (pale yellow)
Achillea verticor yellow (pale yellow)

RED/CRIMSON/PURPLE/CERISE/PINK

Rose 'Jaguar' (red)
Rose 'Mercedes' (red)
Celosia red (red)
Peony (crimson/cerise/pink)
Lupin (substitute Amaranthus red) (crimson)
Hydrangea (pink dries red) (crimson)
Dahlia (purple)
Oregano (purply pink)
Celosia cerise (cerise)
Rose 'Gerdo' (pink)
Rose 'Europa' (pink)
Helichrysum (pink)
Achillea verticor pink (pink)

Useful Addresses

Bailey's Wholesale Floral Supply
P.O. Box 591
Arcadia, IN 46030
Tel: 317/984-3663

Country Road Herb Farm and Gift Barn
1497 Pymatuning Lake Road
Andover, OH 44003
Tel: 216/577-1932

Farmer Ted's Herbs & Everlastings
1349 Pine Ridge
Bushkill, PA 18324
Tel: 717/588-3009

Hummingbird Farm
2041 N. Zylstra Road
Oak Harbor, WA 98277
Tel: 206/679-5044

Lucia's Garden
2942 Virginia Street
Houston, TX 77098
Tel: 713/523-6494

Premier Botanicals Ltd.
8801 Buena Vista Road
Albany, OR 97321
Tel: 503/926-5945
Fax: 503/928-2730

Redding's Country Cabin
Route 1, Box 198-A
Ronda, NC 28670
Tel: 910/984-4070

United Kingdom

The Hop Shop
Castle Farm
Shoreham
Sevenoaks, Kent
Tel: 0959 523 219

Terence Moore Designs
The Barn Workshop
Burleigh Lane
Crawley Down
West Sussex RH10 4LF
Tel: (0342) 717 944

The Herbal Apothecary
103 High Street
Syston, Leicester
Tel: (0533) 602 690

Lesley Hart Dried Flowers
37 Smith Street
Warwick CV34 4JA
Tel: (0926) 490356

Hilliers Garden Centre
Woodhouse Lane
Botley
Southampton SO3 2EZ
Tel: (0489) 782306

Country Style
358 Fulwood Road
Ranmoor
Sheffield S10 3GD
Tel: 0742 309067

Netherlands

W Hogewoning BV
Floralaan 2G
PO Box 265
2230 AG Rijnsburg
Tel: (31) 1718 28501

Star Dried Flowers BV
Floralaan 2A
PO Box 101
2230 AC Rijnsburg

Australia

Flower World
12 Sara Grove
Tottenham
VIC 3012
Tel: (03) 315 2388

Flowerama
Unit 27
8 Gladstone Road
Castle Hill
NSW 2154
Tel: (02) 680 2320

Dominion Agencies
20 Stuart Road
Dulwich
SA 5065
Tel: (08) 332 6688

Valley View Flowers
104 Gavour Road
Wattle Gorve
WA 6107
Tel: (09) 453 6688

New Zealand

Interflora, Head Office
Tel: (0800) 80 88 80
(*Branches nationwide*)

The Florist Group
Auckland City
Tel: (09) 366 7016

Headerish Flowers
Shirley, Christchurch
Tel: (0800) 50 505

Flower Systems Ltd
8 Macklehurst Road
Auckland
Tel: (09) 337 4515

Colleen Murphy Florists
119 Akitchener Road
Milford Square
Tel: (09) 489 5961

South Africa

Honingklip Dry Flowers
13 Lady Anne Avenue
Newlands, Cape Town 7700
Tel: (021) 64-4410

Auckland Park Floral Boutique
7 Seventh Street
Melville, Johannesburg 2092
Tel (011) 726-2116

Peter's Florist
54 First Avenue
Durban 4001
Tel: (031) 309-3439

Index

PLANT INDEX

The plants listed here are those used in this book. We have listed them as they appear, usually by their common name. The botanical name of the plants appear in italics; other common names appear in brackets.

Acknowledgements

The author would like to thank the following:

Jane and Coral for helping get this idea off the ground.

Mike and Diana Steele and Suzanne and Graham Morris for the use of their delightful homes for photography.

Clifton Nurseries, Clifton Villas, London W9 for letting us photograph among their wonderful statues and other garden furniture.

Providence Cabinet Makers, 6 Dry Drayton Industries, Scotland Road, Dry Drayton, Cambridge for the loan of their lovely furniture and other props.

FURTHER READING

Dried Flower Arranger by Alex MacCormick, Severn Hills Book Dist., 1993

Dried Flower Designs by Barbara Laking (ed.), Brooklyn Botanic Gardens, Sterling Books, 1987

Dried Fresh Flowers from your Garden by Elizabeth Bullivant, Viking-Penguin, 1990

The Captured Harvest by Terence Moore, Cassell, 1993

The Pocket Encyclopaedia of Flower Arranging by Malcolm Hillier, Dorling Kindersley, 1990

The Complete Handbook of Garden Plants by Michael Wright, Rainbird Publishing Group, 1984